To all those who offer helpful hints
for the health of the soul and especially
my daughter
Rebecca

ACKNOWLEDGEMENTS

There was never a greater gift than the offer to write a weekly column for a local newspaper. It began as a platform from which to speak to a secular audience about spiritual matters but quickly became a life-line for my own inner peace. Strange. Ten or even five years ago, I would never have described nor thought of myself as a writer. I'd have been amused by the flow of events that leads me to do so now—against all former presuppositions.

Since my childhood, my spelling and syntax have been so poor that various long-suffering teachers cautioned against quitting my day job to take up a literary career. I spelled so poorly, my grade three teacher told me I would never make it to grade four. She was right, for on a test out of 100, I scored -27. Even my own name was incorrect. A tenth grade English instructor sadly remarked that I would never understand the structure of my native tongue if I didn't pay more attention to detail. My doctoral supervisor gently advised me to stick to my passions, since it didn't seem that I was blessed with the patience to hone my writing skills.

I smile now when I look back upon all those teachers who had to push and guide me in the right direction. Some I can no longer name. Impressions are all that remain—the stern look, the pleading glance, the firm exclamation marks. One who does deserve a great deal of credit for pressing me to take care with words is Douglas Hall, the aforementioned doctoral supervisor. His stubborn refusal to accept second-rate goods was the beginning of my journey into the craft.

To all of you, "Thank you!" In some measure, your efforts bore fruit.

More recently, I have been grateful for the invention of "Spell Check" programs which catch my obvious errors and for the doggedness of editors who watch my run-on sentences. Without either, I would, indeed, be a poor excuse for a literary artist. In this regard, I can't express the depth of my appreciation to Dolores Bell who has faithfully edited all of the "hints" offered in this text. Besides the technical support, she has tested each notion against her own firm grasp of reality and often suggested some very helpful alterations.

In a similar fashion, I owe a great deal to Shirley Serviss— a friend, editor and publisher whose attention to detail and creative insight have made this a truly beautiful book. Shirley introduced me to the Alberta writers' community, and their encouragement and interest have been important.

I have crossed paths with many newspaper editors and journalists in recent years. For the most part I have been impressed by their down-to-earth honesty and straightforward critique. For friends at The Edmonton Journal, the paper in which most of these articles appeared, I count myself fortunate to be part of your company, on a weekly basis.

Finally, to Kelly, I owe a debt that cannot be repaid. She has been loyal over many bumps in the road, long-suffering when I was squirrelled away with my computer and lavish in her encouragement.

Christopher Levan
Edmonton, May 1997

TABLE OF CONTENTS

1 Hints for the Healthy Soul

2 The Bible Tells Me So

Out of the Mouths of Babes

Sin Boldly

The Questions You've Always Wanted to Ask

God Loves a Good Story

Religion and Politics

INTRODUCTION

I'm in the soul business, a rather eccentric, though rapidly expanding niche in the economic life of the planet. I began to work in this area in the late '60s before it was trendy or politically correct to "get right with the inner child." In those earlier days, we spoke of a spirit-filled life or a prayerful demeanour. We held "Faith at Work" conferences aimed at teens who wanted to get close to God. Upbeat evangelistic rallies proclaimed the benefits of being a "born again" believer.

But as time passed, most of us saw the soul trade as a declining enterprise, a rear-guard action fighting off the encroachment of a powerfully engaging secular myth of progress. After some initial exposure to our utopian religious ideals, many followers fell off the wagon, got practical, found a profession and forgot about spiritual matters. So passed the '70s and '80s.

Now as the economically constricted '90s come to a close, there is a renewed interest in the pathways of the heart. All the ambition and drive has leaked out of the American dream. With the evident bankruptcy of the secular myth of constant progress, the unemployed and overworked alike are wondering if "this is all there is." Twelve-step programs and food-for-the-soul publications are booming, all promising to reveal the secret "prophecies" of your existence. Make no mistake, there is a religious revolution in the land!

So I should be happy, and most of the time I am. It's gratifying to have one's life work become the focus of public interest. Nevertheless, I am dismayed by some of the hype, publicity and monetary implications which surround certain spiritual quests we are invited to undertake. You see, no matter your religion, you don't need a truckload of money or a well of insight to get in touch with the inner peace you seek. The search for your soul requires just three things: time, honesty and simplicity.

Time! We're a busy race, always so eager for tomorrow that we don't have time for today. There is no fast-food approach to soul hunger. You can't gobble it down on the way to your next appointment. Just as we wouldn't watch a movie or read a book in a couple of minutes, so also with spiritual matters. Slow down. Spirit rest doesn't take years in a monastic cell or even hours on bended knee. The point is to open up your mind and heart to charms of the now. Stop looking over the next horizon or around the bend. Soulful delight begins when we see the beauty that surrounds us and dwells within each person we meet. That may sound corny, but think of spiritual work as a gourmet meal. Savour each mouthful. There is divinity in the air we inhale, in the flowers that surround us. Indeed, in every walk of life, the transcendent is present. We need to take the time to see it and breathe it in.

Honesty! This craft of the heart will be most rewarding if you avoid pretense. The inner soul will not be nourished on cheap hoaxes or quick-fix schemes. Honesty is hard to embrace, for we are a people who thrive on illusions, preferring the guile of special effects to a Monday-to-Friday reality. This is especially true when self-examination is on the menu. Who wants to take off the mask of our own delusions? Let me offer an idea. Look deep into yourself and accept who you are. Of course, we all have warts and wrinkles, so don't be frightened by the unloveable parts of your personality. We are not on this pilgrimage because we are perfect, but to be made whole by bringing all of who we are into harmony.

Simplicity! Now there is a misguided notion that all this spiritual work must be strenuously sobering, if not down right pious. After all, anyone who is on a serious spiritual quest won't have time for frivolous activity or any kind of levity. It's quite the contrary. Spiritual work is like breathing. It works best when we don't obsess about it. Far from stone-cold piety, I believe we come closest to the eternal when we sense a divine folly creeping into our soul.

It is for that reason that I think a simple inner tube is one of the best tools to travel toward the inner soul. It's not so practical in winter weather, but when I am at our summer home and want to restore my spirit, I take a tube ride down the river—no cellular phones please. (They haven't developed a tube with e-mail capabilities, thank heavens.) The pace and peace of the ride can cure countless wounds.

You may think it's silly to paddle down the stream, toes dangling over one side, head laid back on the other. But it's heaven. When I can't actually do it, I replay it in a day dream. Simple. If you're not close to an obliging river, try walking in the woods, hiking in the mountains, lying on a hot sandy beach or soaking luxuriously in the tub.

There are countless pathways to that special spirit-rest and they don't cost a thing. Trust me. I've been in this business a long time and my experience is that what works is often right at heart and in hand.

This selection of stories and ideas is meant to be a helpful companion on your ride down the river, so to speak. They are not intended to be exhaustive on the subject of religion nor do I pretend to be unbiased. They began as an experiment—the attempt to speak of spiritual and ethical matters to a secular audience. Consequently, there is little "Jesus" language, even though I touch on many subjects about which the Christian tradition has a great deal to say. I have generalized these points in order to allow for the interest of a wider readership.

Ironically, and in the end delightfully, the more I tried to address the religious issues of a worldly community, the more clearly I spoke to my own church. Obviously, there are some basic questions which we have been afraid to ask as believers, and a thorough-going examination of them is most helpful.

Through the correspondence which these articles created, I have come to see that no one is without theological insight. Some of the most helpful suggestions came from people with little or no formal theological training, but with clear hearts looking for light. God works in wonderful ways!

This text has been designed to be a quick read—kept by the phone, in the washroom glanced-at-by-visitors basket or by the bedside lamp. Each chapter is a collection of articles which have a similar theme, but they each stand (or fall) on their own merit.

I would like to take credit for the title of this book, but I can't. "Sin boldly" was a piece of advice first coined by Martin Luther. Apparently his second in command, Philipp Melanchthon was prone to nervousness and as the Protestant Reformation took shape, he became more agitated, thinking they were going too far, too fast.   At one point, he came to Luther. In a throwback to his childhood practice of making a confession with a priest, Melanchthon asked his mentor if he would listen to his sins. After the recounting of a number of mouse-size misdemeanours, Luther became agitated. I can imagine him arguing that Melanchthon should go out and do something worth confessing rather than these little vanities he was calling sins. Luther suggested if we, as fallen creatures, were prone to error, we should at least make a dramatic attempt at it. "Sin boldly," were his actual words. God doesn't want whining, religious wimps. Stand up and be counted. Give life a run for its money! As Luther remarked later, God's grace is wide enough to encompass us all, and we should trust in that with equal daring. That's the story. And while we can't be certain of the historical accuracy, there is a great deal of truth in his advice.

1 HINTS FOR THE HEALTHY SOUL

THE PAIN OF LOVING

Why do we love if, in its passing, we hurt so much?

Do you recall your first love? The mind-fogging romance that erased all other thoughts?

Her name was Sheryl, and she sat two rows over and one seat forward in grade three class. Sheryl—my first heartbreak waiting to happen. I can still feel the taunting pangs of that childhood love.

Sheryl was a dark mystery. In my pre-adolescent eyes, other girls were kind, friendly and even attractive. But this curly-haired beauty wielded a special potency. Was it because she came from the other side of town—a world away? Could it have been her stoic unwillingness to speak to any boys on the playground? Maybe I was taken in by her charming accent as she read during English period. No matter. I had a very serious case of infatuation.

I don't believe I said more than a few blush-red greetings to her throughout our one-sided romance. Nevertheless, I counted the hours to Valentine's Day, the one occasion in the school year when I could at least hint at my affections by sending her the big one—the I-LOVE-YOU-WON'T-YOU-BE-MY-VALENTINE card.

Looking back on that hapless child that was me, I am now surprised that I actually did it. I sent my super, guaranteed-never-to-fail valentine and received one in return. Unlike the others from my class, Sheryl's was lace-edged and scented. Well, that clinched it! I was in love. There and then, my destiny was fixed—Sheryl!

The crushing blow came a scant three weeks later when I saw my love, my valentine, walking hand in hand with Roger. How could she betray me so frivolously? Not a second thought nor backward glance. I was toast. Standing in a pool of regret and shame, I vowed then and there I would not set my affections on another being again. It cost too much, cut too deeply.

How many times have you had similar thoughts? Put this book down right now. Go outside and blow the horn on your car for every time you vowed, "Never again!" And if your vehicle's battery wears out before you've finished your litany of "never agains," then welcome to the human race. We all do it —love until it hurts.

Ever wonder why we do it? Why do we love when the losing hurts so much?

While I would never claim to be an expert on loving, I have learned a few lessons. First, loving is like breathing—human beings are made for it. A great sage once argued that our hearts are restless until they can find an object of love. From cradle to grave, we search for those with whom we can express our deepest passions. And many people will never settle down until they have found a "special" someone to love.

There are some pious heros who can turn to God as the object of their love, but many of us also need to see this divine love embodied in another human being. Either way, loving is a natural need—the pain notwithstanding.

Second, love includes pain. It's part of a matched set. Just as love naturally invites us to find great joy in unity with another being, so it also opens us to pain. No one starts out to hurt another, but loving does expose us, leaving us vulnerable. Consequently, deep love renders us deeply helpless before the passions of our beloved. Part of the exhilaration of love is the risk of that openness. Moreover, whether it lasts for a day, a decade or "till death do us part," love in this world will eventually end. So love's blossoming includes its withering. There is a love song which concludes with this lesson, capturing the bittersweet quality of loving. "The first time that we said 'hello' begins our last good-bye." The pain of love's ending is part of the happiness in its beginning. That's the deal.

So, the deeper the love, the deeper the pain. It makes no rational sense. But as Pascal said, "The heart has reasons that reason cannot tell."

Why do we love when in its passing we hurt so much? Some questions are better than any answers. Loving is one such question.

DOES MY DOG HAVE A SOUL?

Sometimes it's a dripping rubber ball that smells like it spent the night in a sewer. Other times it's my soon-to-be-ruined jogging socks, and at still other times, it's a half eaten milk bone from his late night snack. These are the gifts that Frodo, our dog, deposits on our bed early in the morning. Rolling over into them is like a not so subtle wake-up call. "Hello. It's morning, and we haven't gone for a walk around the block yet!"

If these little gifts don't rouse us, then he yawns. In most circumstances, yawning is a sign of impending sleep or boredom, but Frodo yawns with excitement and without ceasing. Like Chinese water torture, if the deposits in the bed don't get us, the yawning always does.

Once downstairs and dressing for our ritual stroll, Frodo acts like it's a new event. What a surprise! A totally novel idea! It doesn't matter that we've done this for three years, four months and fifteen days, and that we've done it in exactly the same manner all of those many mornings—rain or shine, snow or fog. It's fresh and oh so exciting! So what are we waiting for?

Is there something about Frodo's morning ritual which points to a deeper side to creation? For months, I have resisted writing about a dog and his habits because it seemed so mundane. There's nothing spiritual about a pet, for heaven's sake! But as the litany of his yawning continues unabated and each morning we go through the jumping-to-the-ceiling joy of a simple walk down the street, I have come to treasure my dog's soul.

I won't admit it loudly, and it's unlikely to be part of a lecture series, but I believe animals do have souls. Because of our heartless pursuit of empirical knowledge, we are not prone to think of "lesser species" as having anything close to a feeling spirit. We are unable to communicate directly to know how richly other mammals are blessed with a sense of the transcendent, but there seems little doubt that my dog communes with his Creator each morning of his life.

In Frodo's enthusiasm for our walk around the neighbourhood with that first-time-every-time excitement, I sense what I would call the primordial urge of the soul— the desire to be one with our surroundings, to sense again that unity which we knew before we were born.

Do you recall that early period of living when we did not need to boast of our many achievements or climb a corporate ladder? Our self-worth was not tied to our hair style and our salvation to a pay cheque. We just were—no conditions, no exceptions. A life without headaches or heart breaks. Every sensation was as miraculous as it was fresh. In that infantile space, we knew a unity of body and soul. Much of our adult existence is spent trying to regain it. Career and sex and reading and playing—they're all expressions of the quest to find the wholeness that once we enjoyed. If there is one quality of human life that distinguishes us from the created order of plants, birds or even dogs, it is that we know we are separate and alone. That is the burden we bear as cognitive creatures.

It's evening as I write this article, and Frodo is sleeping at my feet—content and oblivious to the perils of the post-modern world. Does he care that the province has a balanced budget? Do the hockey playoffs even enter his mind? He's fed, warm and close to the people who care about him. Peace on earth! But Frodo's calm exterior never fools me. I know that behind his canine slumber is a vital, licking, yawning, yearning spirit which is waiting for morning. Thank goodness for his soul. It brings me back to the real and vital world each time I open my eyes and feel his rubber ball at my back.

THE DANCE OF UNBELIEVING

There are those who write creeds for the beginning of a new year, confessions of faith about life and death. These statements, usually beginning with the bold words "I believe," all too often sound like trumpet calls of triumphant virtue or sentimental hymns of angelic assurance. Believing is a message drummed at us from all sides. "Only believe!" That's the call from the TV evangelist and street corner preacher. These religious salespeople contend that once you have embraced the true faith, your problems will be resolved, your doubts erased and your dreams come true.

It is a pity that we may swallow this reasoning without reflection. How many times have I encountered guilt-ridden people who admit in hushed and penitent tones that they have some grave misgivings about certain religious ideas, and they do not "believe." Whispered burdens of the heart. What a scandal: to be religious and not have faith. Some folk try to emulate the minister, priest or rabbi, seeing her or him as a super hero of belief, able to leap nagging doubts at a single bound, faster than a speeding contradiction. Isn't that what this spiritual exercise is all about—achieving the blessed saint-like stature of a true believer?

I'm an unbeliever and have been all my life. In contrast to the stained glass pronouncements of believing, many of which are desperately shallow or too easy, I have always found that professions of unbelief are satisfying, a tad more honest and an essential part of real faith. Here's why.

Contrary to what you might at first think, unbelieving is an essential step on the journey to lasting belief. Think about it. If I "only believe," without testing my doubts and examining my fears, what is my faith except an empty shell, a house of cards waiting to be blown over at the first sign of resistance? True belief grows from the struggle with doubt and unbelief. Take sickness as an example. When I am feeling healthy, God is not as necessary nor as present to me as God is when I am ill. It is in the moments of help-lessness and darkness that I search most earnestly for answers and assurances. Without the doubt caused by ill health, would I plead to find God with the same sincerity and seriousness?

Unbelieving is also a check against facile credulity. Not every doctrine nor idea merits our belief. Some spirits can deceive us. There once was a great religious thinker who, when asked by a reporter, "Do you believe in the Devil?" replied, "No, never! I can't believe in the Devil. He lies!" Unbelieving is the sober second thought which guards our piety from pretension.

Finally, I turn to my unbelieving as an entry into human frailty and, in a manner I cannot fully comprehend, as a pilgrimage toward God. I feel there is a pain within the heart of God, one caused by human cruelty and injustice. This pain cannot be approached by untroubled statements of belief. Rather, we catch a glimpse of the divine as we travel back and forth along the continuum between doubt and faith, as we wrestle with our virtue and cowardice. God is found, or God finds us, as we undertake that serious struggle. To use an analogy, the divine-human encounter is like a moving stream, not a static event. Unbelieving is the acknowledgement that we have no fixed address; we're always searching, having to plunge in and take our chances.

In the spirit of my unbelief, I offer this list as a guide for the searching soul.

- I unbelieve in money as the power to bring meaning and happiness.
- I unbelieve in efficiency as the measure of all worth.
- I unbelieve in technological progress as the yardstick of human life.
- I unbelieve in work without play.
- I unbelieve in governments that promise dignity while humiliating the poor.
- I unbelieve in building trust funds for a rainy day while people starve.
- I unbelieve in growing old, at least in heart.
- I unbelieve in charity which expects a reward.
- I unbelieve in abuse which masquerades as love and concern.

- I unbelieve in the scolding inner voice within which has forgotten to dance.
- I unbelieve in the finality of death.
- I unbelieve in virtue which must praise itself.
- I unbelieve in evil's simple defeat.
- I unbelieve God has infinite patience with human cruelty.
- I unbelieve life on earth is less important than life in heaven.
- I unbelieve love is easy.
- I unbelieve hope is simple.

What are your unbeliefs?

STAYING IN TOUCH WITHOUT OFFENSE

A recent study indicated that during your garden-variety lunch hour at a public restaurant in Acapulco, Mexicans touch each other 110 times—on average. Parisians, on the other hand, taking the same 60 minute break in the day, touch each other 23 times. I'm not a sociologist nor very clever with numbers, and I'm certainly not a betting man, but I would lay money on the table that in any Earl's restaurants (to use one of our classic Western eating establishments as an example), the lunch time patrons don't touch each other at all—no matter how long they stay for a meal.

By comparison even to the United States, Canada is definitely standoffish—out of touch. It's cold up here, wind-chills drive at exposed flesh. Given the very real need to keep fingers warm and protect the body from freezing, we keep our hands in our pockets. To "stay in touch," northern style means to call each other on the phone.

While I am proud of many aspects of Canadian society, its lack of touching is regrettable. All human creatures are born with a skin hunger. We all yearn to be touched and held, caressed and stroked. Staying in touch is not optional. It's an essential language conveying any number of messages: "I love you!" "I need you!" "I will protect you and heal you!" "You are not alone in your sorrow!" "I understand and will never leave your side!" "I find you attractive!" Having its own vocabulary, touch whispers mysteries beyond words.

In the current atmosphere of suspicion and distrust surrounding physical touching, it is no wonder that we draw back. Men, especially, are called to a greater sensitivity. Yesterday, a friend remarked that he used to be quite a hugger—giving them out to everyone he met, but no longer. "You can get into trouble." That is, indeed, true. While men need to be careful, avoiding the use of touching as control or harassment, I do hope we won't give up on it altogether. Here are a few suggestions for us to remember so that we try to stay in touch without offense.

There seems to be no better starting point than personal awareness. Know who you are and why you're touching someone. It used to be considered a spontaneous gesture, but in these awkward days as we attempt to reorder male-female relations, spontaneity may not be possible. Until it becomes second nature, it is better for men to be clear why they touch. We need to ask ourselves if this embrace or that caress is saying what we intend. Am I "coming on," and do I really want to send that signal? Is this hug a way of saying "congratulations" or "thank you" or "farewell" or "hello?" Let's face it, physical contact is the most powerful communication we have.

For better or for worse, men are also required to exercise greater wisdom than may have been the case in the past. Touching in the workplace may not be as innocent as we imagine. It may be a gesture across power differentials, and that transforms touching, sending a message of control or manipulation we do not intend. The same dynamic is true for touching when there is a clear difference in physical size. Through their sheer bulk, men's bodies can easily intimidate smaller women.

It might well be wiser for people—all people—to ask first and touch second. Some folk are not "in the mood" or comfortable with close physical contact. Just because we are comfortable, does not mean that others are inclined or able to receive a hug in the manner in which it is given. Simply asking makes all the difference and gives people choices and control of their own physical space. This is especially true for small children. Adults just assume that because toddlers are small and cuddly, they have a right to grab or pull them up on their waiting laps. How presumptuous! I suspect we'd be surprised to discover that many of these "close moments" with kiddies are not really experienced that way by the children themselves. Remember the aunt who tweaked your cheek at each greeting and how revolted you felt?

In the final analysis, and appreciating my own best advice, I would risk touching rather than leaving someone isolated. Exercising awareness, wisdom and propriety does not mean that we should silence the physical language. Men need to learn this risking more than women, since "keeping in touch" is difficult for us. We often construe same-gender touching as sexual or "weird." How pitiable if we can't hug or hold our fathers, for instance, to express a love and friendship which is genuine and deep.

So, take a settling breath and take a chance. There are some situations—deep grief, broken dreams, lost jobs, death and suffering when touch is the only word we can speak, the only way we can hear. It is far better to err by touching and being rebuffed, than to stand aloof and watch the pain of another multiply because, at the very moment when they need to be joined to another soul— they are out of touch.

REGRET AND HOW WE DON'T DEAL WITH IT

Can someone tell me where I will find the office of "Grieving Regret?" I'm dragging around a truckload of it and would like to park it somewhere. The telephone directory's blue pages list countless government services. There's an office for provincial parks, a road conditions help-line, even a bureau for oversized trucks. I have the number for the deeds registry and the small claims court, but there is no mention of "regrets." Where do I lie them down?

Technology has improved our access to emergency assistance, but there's no mention of what to do in case of an attack of deep regretting. You can dial 911 when fire strikes or if poisonous substances trouble you. A touch of the dial and the ambulance will be at your door, the police not far behind. There's a rape crisis line listed, and even a number to call if I dig up a sunken cable. But what about some place to bury my regrets?

And let's not forget the self-help groups. We have so many in the city that there is a special phone directory dedicated just to them. There's a Compulsive Overeaters Support Group, and a whole host of substance abuse symposiums: Alcohol Anonymous prototypes. I found the listing for WISH, a Widowed in Search of Hope group. If you've got Fibromylagia, heart disorders, or Parkinson's disease you can find a place for unburdening your soul, but what about me—isn't there something like Regretters Anonymous?

Why the mad search for a place to express my grieving regret? It arose for me again when I went to see the movie, "Mrs. Doubtfire." If you haven't seen it, I won't spoil the plot. The story revolves around a family in crisis, and much like "Ordinary People," it tries to paint a realistic picture of the tangle of emotions brought to the surface when one parent leaves home and children. I want to commend the producers of this film because they don't give in to a Hollywood ending—the American style "they all lived happily ever after" resolution. In real life, some people don't live happily ever after. Many children, indeed close to half the little people of this culture, live in homes other than the "traditional" two-biological-parent variety. Aside from the humour and entertainment value of "Mrs. Doubtfire," its worth rests in its straight-shooting, yet comforting message of acceptance. No matter how your family looks, strange as it may appear when compared to the "norm," it is a family, and you are complete and loveable. Great sentiments! We need more such expressions!

Nevertheless, in spite of all its assurances, the movie dredged up my deep, grieving regret that things are not the way I had once imagined they would or should be. My family did not follow the prescribed pattern.

Here's the "regret" predicament facing all those who live in blending, bending or broken families. While your children may not want the old situation back (the biological mom and dad under the same roof and their fights and tension), they also regret deeply that both their parents are not living with them. The same is also true for the adults.

You know you can't go back to a relationship which was abusive, twisted or just plain dead. Nevertheless, you regret that you and your children are not experiencing the "normal" secure family life they were lead to believe they should have.

I call this "grieving regret" because it goes beyond the sense of remorse or sorrow. I send my "regrets" when I can't be at a meeting. I'll get there next time, after all, so there's no lasting problem. The emotion I feel over disrupted homes is akin to grief. Something has died and can't be revived. That's a fact which won't go away with time and can't really be repaired, no matter how much child support we give or how many hours of quality parenting we spend. We will drag this regret with us always.

Regret is not life-threatening, and that's the problem. There's no need for an emergency service for regretters. I don't need a 24-hour intervention or even weekly reassurances. Regret is not bad—but it lasts forever. Like a mildly toxic emotion, it takes a very long time to biodegrade. It is a low level yearning that seeks an outlet from time to time, a place to confess itself, lay down the burden and then carry on.

In past societies, we had ceremonies and symbols which helped people deal with their regret. Christians established Ash Wednesday and Good Friday for that purpose. The Jewish community celebrates Yom Kippur. Islamic cultures have a similar custom. While these special days and ceremonies still exist, there is a great gapping need in a society which is becoming more secular as each year passes. Perhaps it's time for the civic authorities to reflect on a means for dealing with regret—a day set aside, a ribbon campaign, a ceremony.

Maybe we should just show "Mrs. Doubtfire" every New Year's Eve. In the end, laughter, mingling with our tears, may be the only antidote for deep regret.

NATIONAL FOOT-WASHING WEEK

Amidst the blaze of government induced budget-bashing bravado, you may have missed National Hand-Washing Awareness Week. It happened for seven days beginning February 20 and was promoted as a conscience-raising, educational event. Medical research is now clear and emphatic. Washing your hands carefully does prevent illness and the spread of infectious diseases.

Promoters of National Hand-Washing Awareness Week hosted free hand-washing clinics, instructed school children in the art of proper hand washing, and called on the public to make a clean break from unsanitary habits. According to those who have studied such matters, it takes 20 seconds of hand-wringing in your average warm, soapy water for germs and other disease carrying grease and grime to be removed thoroughly from your hands. Advocates of this unique awareness program suggested that children could sing through their ABCs while washing in order to know when 20 seconds was up. Unfortunately, I did not hear if there was a comparable song that adults could employ while performing their ablutions. Maybe a round of "I Did It My Way."

Do I sound cynical? Well, ... just a bit. Do you have a feeling that almost every day of the year has become a special day designated for everything from family fellowship to animal rights? Like many, I have trouble keeping up with the special flavour of the week. Nevertheless, National Hand-Washing Awareness Week did spark an inspiration for me—not about hands, but feet.

I come from a religious tradition in which foot washing is more than personal hygiene. It is also regarded as a symbolic act of servanthood and hospitality, a very moving and deeply spiritual experience gathering together many threads which run through the fabric of religious practice: trusting, cleansing, risking, healing and forgiving. According to legend, disciples of Jesus would gather on regular days and wash each other's feet. For a time, this common action rivalled the other early sacraments of communion and baptism. While it fell into disuse and was almost lost, foot washing is experiencing a revival. Many Christian churches now incorporate this worshipful act during their Holy Week services. Another pathway to the holy. You could call it sole food!

Here's my pitch. Why can't foot washing be raised to the level of a secular pastime or non-religious gift of affection? We enjoy hot tubs. How about foot tubs? Our feet are, after all, the most neglected part of the anatomy and yet the most overworked and underpaid. Unlike hands, our feet are regularly crammed into tight spaces, covered in a dank, often foul-smelling cloth, and subjected to indiscriminate changes in temperature, sometimes hot and dry, other times cold and wet. Don't you think we'd all be better off, more productive and freed from undue stress if we paid them a little attention? Reflexologists (practitioners of therapeutic foot massage) argue that our feet are central to the healthy rhythm of our bodies. These alternate health care workers suggest that many of the body's ills can be altered if not cured through massage and tender care of our feet.

Imagine what could happen on a National Foot-Washing Awareness Week:

- Couples could agree to wash each other's feet each evening. A hot steamy tub of water, a portion of Epsom salts and you have your own miniature jacuzzi—at a fraction of the cost. I predict the contentment quotient of our community would rise dramatically in that one week. People would be coming to work with a milky, mellow smile instead of sharp shrugs.

- Campaigns could be mounted to have foot-washing basins installed in our workplaces. By state legislation, it would be mandatory as a once-a-week work benefit. If its effects are even half as productive in the office as they are at home, there's no reason why the government couldn't consider regular foot washing as a deficit-saving measure.

- Entrepreneurial competitions could be mounted. There may be a whole new field of service opening up for the unemployed. Right beside the neighbour-hood tanning salons, we'd have new foot-washing parlours. Picture yourself looking for a break after having walked through the mall for hours. Presto! There is the foot-washing clinic. A 15-minute pause, some gentle rubbing and scrubbing on those tired tootsies and you're ready to shop 'till you drop.

Alright, my imagination can get out-of-hand (or should I say out-of-foot?), but I have no doubt that in a rushed and bustling world, we need simple acts of affection and com-passion, inexpensive ways to say I love and I care.

Let's hear it for National Foot-Washing Awareness Week. It starts on any day you like. Right now. Just put your best foot forward.

FORGIVENESS IS GOD'S WORK

Forgiveness is a fearful tool in the hands of an amateur. When I was seven years old I was part of my one and only schoolyard brawl. I can no longer recall the burning reason that caused me to leap off the bike rack onto Tommy Smyth's back, but I knocked him down and rubbed his face in snow. With calculated disdain, I gobbed on his forehead and inadvertently pushed his glasses off his prominent round nose. The end result was that I broke his spectacles and our friendship.

Guilty! You can't imagine how badly I felt. Tommy would never speak to me again, and my life would be stalked by the fear of reprisals from his gang. Besides any earthly concerns, I waited all day for a divine intervention. Surely the heavens would open up and a lightning bolt would flash down to strike me dead. My Maker would visit retribution upon me for such a dreadful act.

Apparently, God does not view the breaking of visual aids as a crime or was busy elsewhere. Whatever the reason, I neither heard nor felt any celestial punishment on that or any subsequent day.

In a week, Tommy got a new pair of glasses and in about a month, he told me he was ready to forgive. My heart lightened. "I will forgive you, " he intoned from the hilltop of his righteousness, "if you will carry my lunch for the rest of year and wash my bike next Tuesday." It was forgiveness all right, but it was forgiveness with a catch. Alas, with the unskilled, there's always a catch. I could enjoy restoration into Tommy's good graces but only if I showed myself to be duly penitent and grateful.

It's because we are amateurs that we can't handle forgiveness like a professional. After all, forgiveness is essentially God's work. We mortals are merely mimicking the Almighty when we seek to offer forgiveness. All too often our forgiveness comes with a hook. Tommy had been injured, he wanted to make me pay, and he did his accounting using the weapon of forgiveness. How could I turn him down? How could I cry foul? He was the injured party and now he was being magnanimous by making me an offer to set things right. Why didn't I feel relieved? Well, I felt that his forgiveness was a manipulative measure—designed to make me suffer for his acceptance. It didn't set me free or give me a sense of restoration, but ground my face into my misdeed.

Forgiveness, in the biblical sense, is without condition. It does not expect anything but is simply an offer to allow someone back into communion. Certainly Jesus' forgiveness was given in that manner. In human affairs, we have suffered from a confusion, believing that forgiveness was the way to make things right, to solve problems. But in fact, forgiveness is a free agent, not tied to forgetting or receiving anything.

In other words, forgiveness is not the beginning of restitution, but its conclusion. Healthy human relationships are based on justice, not forgiveness. Justice implies that every human being has their just desserts, their fair share of the gifts which the world has to offer. As creatures of a loving God, our primary task is to establish justice in our communities. Those folk who are injured should not be expected to forgive, but they can expect justice, the state in which their injury is redressed or at least compensated.

The whole notion of forgiving and forgetting is sentimental hogwash. Some crimes are not forgivable by human standards, and many calamities cannot be forgotten. So when we deal with each other, we should be seeking to establish just relationships—not an easy job by any means, but certainly within our grasp. It is only on the basis of this justice that we can all become healthy.

In contrast to justice-making, true forgiveness, the kind that is not contingent, is more like a miracle, an unexpected gift which arises from the security people feel when justice is truly established on earth. It cannot be legislated nor forced—it is God's act. Like love, forgiveness is a free flowing offer—with a one-way direction. It does not demand nor seek a return, otherwise it is not forgiveness.

God save us from the people who would use forgiveness for their own ends—to make us "good" or bring us back to the fold, or curb our behaviour in some way.

THE ONE THING I FORGOT

The tent is up and the bedroll is laid neatly on the air mattress. Now I can relax by the picnic table and breathe in the fresh fragrances of God's wilderness. The bugs are co-operating and all will be well. It's my first trek into the woods for this season, and I can't wait for that oh-so-mellow feeling to overtake my commute-to-the-office weary soul. Just between the marshmallows and the late night stroll to the showers, the weight of city life will slip from my shoulders and I will know peace.

There is, however, something about the first tenting trip—a built-in default button—which always makes me overlook something. Each year I promise myself I will not forget anything, and each time I unpack the car—there it isn't. Last year it was the flashlight (what a time we had bumping off to the outhouse late at night). The year before, a pair of oven mitts were left behind (a pity, since we had nothing with which to snatch the red hot frying pan from the camp fire). My family won't let me live down the time I dragged them all up a two-hour slope in order to enjoy a mountain wiener roast, only to discover I left the hot dogs on the kitchen counter. Once, I left the tent at home—a minor detail on a tenting vacation. This time, I discovered I forgot the groundsheet. How could I forget such an essential piece of equipment? Most times that wouldn't matter, but with the rains this summer, it does.

Why am I telling you this? You're probably not close enough to lend me a groundsheet, even if you had one. Actually, it strikes me, as I sit here in my slightly damp tent, that life is like my camping trip. There is always something missing, a minor or major detail. It is the rare person who has it all, remembers everything, who never misses a beat or who doesn't misplace a crucial item.

There are, of course, many Madison Avenue types (the high priests of our consumptive society) who would want us to believe that the perfect life is out there some-where if we would just try a little harder and spend a little more. Religious gurus aren't beyond this kind of presumption either. There's always a preacher somewhere who will promise you the perfect life in exchange for a few well-rehearsed credal affirmations. Aside from these blatant evangelists, the religious enterprise promotes perfection by inference only. Rather than being a bold sign at the front door, it's more like an unspoken assumption. People who go to church or synagogue or mosque or temple have their act together. Right? Of course, right! You wouldn't find them with a misplaced moral or a dangling virtue. They have it all worked out.

How often have I sat through worship looking at others and wondering how they do it. Is it possible to be so calm and collected? There are many times when I try to pretend that I also have a perfect, well-put together existence—missing ground sheets notwithstanding. But this show requires a good deal of energy and not a small amount of denial and deceit.

Let's take a deep breath. Life is, indeed, like a camping trip because there is no complete or altogether life. Everyone suffers loss and pain and doubt, and no one has the corner on virtue. The trick is to relax and accept what we have been given and struggle through the hours with what we have not been given—like being in the middle of the wilderness without a groundsheet. There are no second takes, no stores close by that sell us the emotions or brains we lack. There isn't anything you can do but laugh a little at our own silly, lovable selves and enjoy the scenery. After all, isn't that what God does?

THE BLESSINGS AND CURSES OF GROWING OLD

I hate growing older. Nothing is ever so clear again once you pass 40.

Barney the TV dinosaur, Superman and the Tooth Fairy all have one thing in common. They know what they're all about. They have no doubts, not a quiver in their voices nor hesitation in their steps. They know what's good and what's bad, and without a second thought they do good. In fact, they live and breathe and even sleep goodness. It's no big deal. They just know it and do it.

I used to know too. In another age, before I passed the midpoint mark in my life, I could spout off about righteousness at the drop of a hat. Like St. Nick, I could see when I had been bad or good, and I was "good for goodness sake."

But now, I don't know anymore. The good seems to be more elusive; just when I imagine that it is within my grasp, it dissolves. We finish reading a stirring novel, only to discover the author beats his wife. We catch a breathtaking song on the radio and later learn that the singer is charged with numerous drug-related crimes. Inspiring politicians and sports heros turn out to have shady sides and ulterior motives. Even the once unquestionably good and holy men of religion are revealed to be child abusers or power mongers.

It's happening too often now to ignore. I once could pretend that these disappointments were just blips on the screen, what Star Trek characters might call "cosmic anomalies." But let's face it, when the knights in shining armour turn their backs, they look clouded and grey. The good is transitory. Maybe it was just an illusion, a bad joke. It is the curse of my maturing eyes to see ambiguity so clearly, to know that everyone talks about being good but very few seem to do it fully. There are some industrial strength disappointments to the maturing process!

When I am caught by this brand of despair, I think of noble, hapless King Arthur. Have you seen the Camelot movie with Sean Connery? Most of us know the plot and the characters from memory. An unblemished monarch is betrayed by his best friend, a man who had sworn to uphold goodness at all costs. A great, dare I say, heavenly vision will be slimed by the greed and lust of a mere mortal.

Camelot's lasting appeal resides largely in its portrayal of how really "good" people perform miserably, deny their virtuous principles and muck about in evil ways. It is wonderfully real, a story of human tragedy writ large. When the final betrayal comes and it seems evident that darkness has overcome the light, Arthur laments, dreaming of the time that was. Though an inner voice urges him to surrender to a sour-as-grapes bitterness, he waits in hope. After all that has befallen his great achievements, he still believes that somewhere Camelot will be born again. He can't predict where, but he knows it will happen someday.

We might argue that Arthur is a foolish man. Surely he, more than anyone else, should know that goodness is an illusion. It is as nonexistent in seventh century Britain as in 20th century North America. But just a minute—the good old king may be wiser than we suspect at first glance. First, he has learned the hard way, as many of us do, that goodness is not as easy to achieve as it may seem. And he has discovered, through painful experience, that no one is entirely good. Each human being has a dark side.

First of all, unlike Barney, Superman or the Tooth Fairy, human aging is that process when we, like Arthur, learn to live with our own limits and with the knowledge of how broken, dark and misshapen the human soul can become. Hey...we're not perfect, and the sooner we realize that fact, the more real and content we become. Second, Arthur appreciates the importance of dreaming, of hoping for a day when goodness will blossom again. It may be foolish to imagine that anyone is totally virtuous, but it is equally naive to assume that evil will always triumph. For the night does not endure forever. Dawn will come as surely as the sun will rise. The good that resides in every human heart will bloom again and take root. It takes a particular kind of patience to water it and wait for it to grow. Arthur had that patience.

As we mature in years, that is one blessing we inherit—the patience to dream beyond our blemishes to the great possibilities that await around the corner. Having said all that, I still hate growing older!

CAN YOU BUY REALITY?

"Get real!" That's what we say when we sense a false note in our relationships with others. But what do we mean? What is real?

That's not an easy question these days. Nevertheless, if you have five dollars, you can get an answer. There's a technological response to that ancient quest for the real—a new generation of video games called "virtual reality." At five dollars a play, it's cheap wisdom. You can now find it in or beside most video arcades. Thousands of young people pay big bucks to spend their idle hours hooked up to a human-size gyroscope. With the help of highly sophisticated masks and gloves, they enter into a non-existent, electronically simulated world that looks and feels, even smells, like the real thing.

For those of us who haven't ventured into this unreal world, here's how it works. According to my son, who is a "virtual reality" aficionado, you move and feel and touch a world which the computer constructs around you—a gunfight, a ball game, a walk in the park. As you move your mask, the program adjusts the picture to imitate panoramic vision. Reach with your hand to touch a flower and the glove gives you the sensation of soft petals. The technology is designed to recreate the experience of reality. Marvellous! Miraculous!

Why? Why would people pay to "experience the real" when they can do it for nothing? You don't have to line up for "real reality." It's there waiting for you when you open your eyes in the morning. There's no need for electronics or delicately balanced computer programs. A simple heart-beat will do. Why would we leave the actually real for the artificial? Why the escape?

Perhaps we escape because, like many people who have gone before us, we are frightened by the rough edges of living—cancer, sexual abuse, poverty, war. They cut deeply into our security and comfort. Maybe we long to avoid the nasty cruelty of injustice which reality promises for so many—the black, the homosexual, the woman, the aboriginal, the welfare recipient. Escape is certainly an easy solution when reality is difficult to fathom. In the culture of immediate gratification, we can't wait to be real. Besides, we who grew up on television images of the "happy ever after" ending may prefer a reality we can control. We prefer it with an on/off button. Who wants the real world when it seems so weather-worn and ambiguous by comparison?

In response to this encroaching escapism, I could quote scripture or uncover some wise Buddhist-like admonition to patience. But Margery Williams in her short book, The Velveteen Rabbit, points most clearly to the hardship, the hurts and joys of what it means to be real. Two toys are talking with each other about their life and the newest, a toy rabbit, asks our question.

"What is REAL?" asked the Rabbit one day when they were lying side by side near the nursery fender before Nana came to tidy the room. "Does it mean having things that buzz inside you and a stick-out handle?"

"Real isn't how you're made," said the Skin Horse. "It's a thing that happens to you. When a child loves you for a long, long time, not just to play with, but REALLY loves you, then you become Real."

"Does it hurt?" asked the Rabbit.

"Sometimes," said the Skin Horse, for he was always truthful. "When you are Real, you don't mind being hurt."

"Does it happen all at once like being wound up," he asked, "or bit by bit?"

"It doesn't happen all at once," said the Skin Horse. "You become. It takes a long time. That's why it doesn't often happen to people who break easily, or have sharp edges, or who have to be carefully kept. Generally, by the time you are Real, most of your hair has been loved off, and your eyes drop out and you get loose in the joints and very shabby. But these things don't matter at all, because once you are Real, you can't be ugly, except to people who don't understand."

"Real" can't be bought, not for five dollars nor a fortune. You don't "get real." It's given to you through shared love and compassion.

DON'T WAIT FOR THE RIGHT TIME

Gridlock downtown on a Friday afternoon. I'm looking at my watch. The seconds are ticking by, and I should have been back at the office seven minutes ago to meet a guest. The cars ahead seem to have grown anchors. Mired in the exhaust, they appear stuck and immovable. Little snippets of summertime wisdom on the radio don't help, and I can feel my temperature rising along with the heatwaves from the pavement.

A faint echo from one of those management seminars comes back to me: "Never let a client cool their heels because you are unable to be on time!" After all, it's not as though there aren't enough clocks around. Old two-armed bandits, digital displays, computer-generated images—you can hardly escape knowing what time it is!

Is it my fault I live in a world that is racing the sweep of time? There must be a better way to live, some calmer relationship to the passing of the hours.

There is a famous piece of scripture which was written for our culture and for a people bent upon beating the sun to the end of the day. Made famous by the folk singers of the '70s, it goes like this:

To everything there is a season,
  and a time for everything under heaven;
a time to be born, and a time to die;
a time to plant, and a time to pluck up what is planted;
a time to kill, and a time to heal;
a time to break down, and a time to build up...

The list continues until almost nothing is missing. No, the writer makes no mention of writing e-mail reports nor returning telephone messages nor even cutting the grass, but the point is pretty clear. Your life has been given to you with enough time to do all that is required of you. Don't fret! Each moment is filled with the potential for meaning if we are willing to see it within a pattern. Even the traffic jam is a message.

Contrary to what you might think, this bible text is not about finding the laid-back golden age, nor an invitation to retreat into a soulful peace, free from the horns and the headaches of this traffic jam called modernity. The life of the one who wrote that advice was just as filled with necessity as our own. Food was not available at the corner store, and each year's crop was literally a matter of survival or destitution. There were no police forces; you were on your own when it came to protection. All too often, those people who were supposedly your shield against aggression were the aggressors themselves. The scripture writer wanted us to see our lives as part of a larger whole, to recognize that all events fall within a design. Call it providence or destiny, according to the testimony of the Bible, God has not abandoned history, but is present in every ticking minute.

That may sound naive until you get behind the surface questions of how and where. First, time is not empty. Scriptures argue that each second is filled with the potential of transcendence. There isn't anywhere nor any time when you can be separated from the possibility of living a new life, of feeling that you are loved and accepted by your Creator. In everything under heaven—at the bedside, grave side, curbside—God is with us. Second, don't think of God as appearing always like a mighty angel. Sometimes He's the flush warmth when a small child holds our hand; other times, She's that little whispered word of welcome. God might even be in this traffic jam.

In fact, you could play God right now. Why not relax your jaw, loosen your grip on the wheel and let those tight-faced people in the car up ahead into your lane. Go ahead. Take the time to smile at them and wave them on. Believe me, then they will really begin to believe in miracles—and perhaps even God.

HAVING ENOUGH— THE DAILY BREAD SOLUTION

So are we happy yet? A recent poll reported that we're not. Fewer than half of Canada's adults, 47 percent in fact, believe they are better off than their parents. That's quite a drop from the 75 percent who thought that way in 1989. Evidently, a majority of Canadians believe they're poorer than past generations. In spite of the inflation-adjusted reality that our average incomes have more than doubled since our fathers were the wage earners (mothers weren't a dominant factor in the paid workforce of the day), we're discontented. I imagine we could find similar figures for Americans.

We obviously haven't noticed the change in our pay envelopes. Rolling down the slippery perception of unattainable ambitions, we're miserable. Look at us. On the Monday to Friday treadmill, both parents putting in overtime like there was no tomorrow, many teenagers in the family unit supplementing the household income with part-time jobs, and it seems that we're still no closer to the goal of security and contentment. It is true that as individuals our debt loads have increased. So it's not simply an urban myth that we're further from the nirvana of a balanced domestic budget and peace of mind. It just takes a lot of money to survive in this no-money-down society. Is it any wonder we're miserable?

Of course, the problem is not low salaries, but our rapidly rising expectations. Boomers grew up in an age of unprecedented growth. The years from 1950 to 1960 were a faster-than-speeding-bullet anomaly on an otherwise slow-moving economic train. The shower of blessings felt good to us back then when we were kids. It was a go-for-broke-'cause-there's-more-where-that-came-from dream. The trouble is that we're still living with that full-throttle mentality, even though the caravan has slowed to a crawl. While average incomes are up, consumption is out of control. Is there no limit to our possessive spirit? Modern houses have more bells and whistles than the space shuttle, and, consequently, purchasing one incurs a greater debt. Leisure activity expenses have gone into orbit. If you're hungry for education, it almost requires a mortgage arrangement. Owning a car is like selling your soul for 48 months. Even penny candy now costs a quarter. Is it any surprise that our possessive spirit has made us the most indebted culture in this century, perhaps in the history of civilization?

This appetite takes some effort to fulfil. Quite naturally there is less time available for real living as we spend our sleepless nights counting up unpaid bills.Yes, we're miserable for some very good reasons. The financial gurus will, no doubt, offer many economic solutions to this predicament. Invest smarter, work more efficiently, shop around for the best interest rate, consolidate loans, lease rather than buy vehicles. Some of this advice is indeed helpful, but happiness is not found in the cheque book. It begins with the state of your soul.

Does that sound too simplistic? Of course, there are those practitioners of religion who will argue that if you get right with God all things will work out for the best. Just pray and you'll be fine. That's not my point. Happiness is the spiritual state when, as much as possible, we are free of this damned possessing spirit. Our problem is not economic, not a question of increasing revenues, but decreasing or altering our expectations.

The bible offers a rather novel approach to the problem of growth. It's called the "Sabbath." Now we often think of a sabbath as a day of rest, but what if you thought of it as being synonymous with the principle of "enough"?

In the Hebrew scriptures God works for six days and then takes a break on the seventh, saying that's enough. Take a break.

Can we take that same attitude to living the daily bread approach where we seek only that which we need for the day? Is it possible for us to plan a reduction in our expectations, to live into a space where we need less—just enough?

The sabbath mentality is sorely lacking in this whining culture of consumers. Would it not honour what our parents have done for us if the boomer generation declared a sabbath, an age of enough. It boils down to my grandmother's dictum: "Happiness is wanting what you have, not having what you want."

2 THE BIBLE TELLS ME SO

YOU CAN'T USE THE BIBLE AS A RULE BOOK

The National Hockey League has an official rule book—pages and pages of instructions for what a professional player can and can't do on and even off the ice. Football, soccer, baseball, basketball—almost every sport has its authoritative collection of regulations, a concise code to govern the play.

What about life—is there a rule book to which we can turn when we get in trouble, when someone is elbowing us in the corner of our pain, tripping us just as we're about to break free? What happens when, in the day-to-day grind, someone is injured by unsportsmanlike conduct? Where do we turn for justice, to discover the statutes or rules which make living manageable and orderly?

If you get a chance to see the movie "Philadelphia," you'll discover that one of the main characters, a high-flying lawyer, has found his book of rules for life. When being questioned about homosexuality, AIDS and proper human behaviour, he has no trouble citing laws, knowing what is right and wrong or identifying the many codes that govern his life. What is his source? The bible, of course. According to the lawyer, that text contains all the commandments, formulas and regulations that any human being can possibly need. This is not an uncommon perception. Many believers turn the holy scriptures into a rule book for the game of life.

What an inappropriate and potentially misguided use of the bible! The Hebrew scriptures and the Christian scriptures were not written primarily as codes for human behaviour—they're not a rule book. They are first and foremost testimonies to people's faith in an actively compassionate Creator. The commandments are clearly derivative and secondary to the central proclamation that God is One and God is loving.

Take the question of homosexuality as an example. Often when Christians debate the appropriateness of same-sex relationships or lifestyles, they quote scripture, believing that citing a disparaging verse from Leviticus or Romans resolves the issue—gives us a rule: "homosexuality is a sin."

While such a "proof texting" has an appealing, common sense quality, it is inadequate when facing the complexity of current questions. Regarding homosexuality, there is a major difficulty confronting those who would claim to read the entire bible and follow it like a set of regulations for living. These folk must ask themselves why they have chosen to ignore certain parts of scripture, some very clear and detailed rules, while latching tenaciously onto the ones about homosexual behaviour.

For instance, there are several rather "interesting" laws about not mixing substances. Leviticus 19:19 forbids the mingling of different seeds in sowing or the mixing of linen with wool in the fabrication of garments. Look at your sweater label—maybe you're sinning without knowing it. Or what happened to the economic commandments of Deuteronomy 15:1 which declare that every creditor shall write off all loans in the seventh year.

Mortgages are to be forgiven as well. Wouldn't that work wonders for our banking system! Then turn to Paul's first letter to the church in Corinth where in chapter 14:34 he directs that women should remain silent in church assemblies for "it is a shame for women to speak in the church." I don't know any self-respecting Christian community of faith that would try to impose that rule. Why do we ignore these other regulations and yet hold fast to the ones on certain sexual behaviour? There's a second problem with relying on the bible as a code book to direct us, giving us hard and fast laws by which to live. Often, the scripture's view of what is important runs contrary to our own. On the question of homosexuality again, it is clear that the bible doesn't consider it to be important at all. At the very outside, there are seven or eight references to male homosexual behaviour, only one vague phrase referring to females who seek the company of other women. In a book of many thousands of rules, hundreds of pages, scores of poems, homosexuality is a very small matter indeed, so small as to be irrelevant. The ancient Hebrew language doesn't even have a word for homosexual and never mentions the possibility of lesbianism. So how can we make a claim that a handful of verses constitute the basis on which to make an ethical judgement about gays and lesbians?

Some would respond—that homosexuality is such an obvious affront to God that we don't need more than a few lines to direct us. One must be careful when advancing that argument. The bible says a great deal in favour of slavery, condoning it often, directing their care and protection. And yet, we have considered slavery to be such an obvious contradiction of God's love and justice that we have ignored all that the bible has to say in its defence. Quite obviously, believers have been selective in their reading of the rules in the bible, prejudicing their choice by cultural and societal standards. We have used our human judgment to suspend certain clear biblical imperatives. Many churches have taken a similar course with respect to the holy book's patriarchal injunctions against women. Why can't the same thinking be applied to the treatment of homosexuals? There may be many people who have difficulty accepting the "naturalness" or "health" of such relationships, but it is unjust to bring those particular opinions to the biblical record and find what you're looking for there.

Oh, you can peer into scriptures and see what you want. No question. But will it be a faithful use of God's word and a faithful response to the question at hand? There once was a great Christian preacher who said the bible is a bit like a mirror: "If a jackass looks in, can we expect a saint to look out?"

FACT OR TRUTH: WHO IS JESUS?

The Jesus wars are heating up. Imagine fighting over a figure who lived 2000 years ago, but scholars from the left and right are lining up across the great divide. "Who is Jesus?" they ask. Answers are quite varied. Some argue that he was an itinerant healer and preacher who attacked the temple and was subsequently crucified by the Romans. On the opposite side, others maintain that Jesus was the self-aware son of God who used divine power to cure the sick and feed the hungry and after his death ascended into heaven to be with his Creator. Was he human? Was he divine?

Ho-hum—religious leaders were arguing over that in the third century. What was a tired and tattered debate has suddenly found new life. Both Time and Newsweek run cover stories on the question of the historicity of Jesus of Nazareth. What makes this newsworthy is the insistence of a group of scholars, known as the Jesus Seminar, that we can know more about the life and times of Jesus than once thought possible.

By studying the cultural and social dynamics of the Mediterranean world of that period, archaeologists and historians are reconstructing a convincing picture of the life in that context. By extension, they are able to re-think many of the sayings and deeds of Jesus. In the process, some fairly orthodox ideas are being questioned. Was he really born in Bethlehem? Did Jesus really say, "I am the resurrection and the life?" Could there have been a trial of Jesus before Pilate? Did the resurrection really happen as it is described in the gospels?

In many ways, the current discussion boils down to a single point. Is there a difference between fact and truth? That is not a rhetorical question. Repeat it to yourself several times because it may be hard to understand at first glance. Why not take a stroll around the block and let your mind percolate on the problem.

Here's the issue. Our modern scientific world has too easily equated historicity with veracity. So when we hear a fairy tale and ask if it is a "true" story, we want to know if the events described actually took place. Consequently, when people ask if the Jesus story is "true" they question if the parables, sayings and deeds of this messiah figure are historically accurate.

The conflict arises when we recognize that the gospels do not all tell the same story. A quick survey of the resurrection stories of Matthew, Mark, Luke and John indicates a great disparity in the record. Which writer do you credit with having the facts right? Moreover, these texts have been interpreted for such a long time by Christians who wanted the story to be considered factual, it is very difficult, if not impossible, to get behind the testimony of believers to the kernel of historical events. Most scholars now agree that there is very little in the Jesus story which we can claim has the stamp of what modern critics might call "historical fact." Let's face it, the gospels were written not as history books, but rather as proclamations of faith.

It's impossible to prove the facts about Jesus and his divinity, so we shouldn't be surprised at the present impasse. The declaration that Jesus is the only begotten son of God is a statement of truth, not fact.

Just because we cannot pinpoint every fact in the story, does not mean it is devoid of truth. For instance, take a look at the now-famous picture of the founders of Canada meeting in the Charlottetown, Prince Edward Island. Now ask yourself if this is a truthful rendition of that conference held in 1864. Most people would reply, "yes." There was, indeed, a gathering of these very people in that place. Out of their deliberations we created Canada. The picture is, therefore, a truthful rendition of the event. But did these men actually sit in these poses, waiting for their images to be put to canvas? The answer is "no." There was no historical moment when Sir John A. held the charter in hand while George Etien looked on in subdued reverence. The picture is a representative image, the fabrication of an artist. It's not factual, even though it is true.

It sounds a bit bizarre, but if we look at the decisions of our daily life, it's evident that we make many more choices on the basis of what we consider to be the truth, rather than on what we know is fact. For instance, how many hockey tickets are sold to fans because they "believe" their team is the best in the league? How many restaurants depend on the business created by couples who feel they have found their "one and only"? Truth is what we live by, not fact. To get back to the bible, while I can't accept the gospel accounts of Jesus as factual, I believe what is said about him as the special revelation of God is true.

What do you think?

HONOUR THY FATHER AND THY MOTHER

Do I honour my father if he sexually abuses me? How can I muster anything like dutiful trust if my mother abandons me? Am I sinful if I hate or even denounce my parents? We all grew up with the ten commandments, but as adult life grows in ambiguity, these written-in-stone laws are less and less helpful. Take the fifth as an example. It clearly says that I am to "honour my father and mother." According to the bible, my well-being, social standing and longevity are dependent on strict adherence to that rule. But what if my parents are abusive to me?

Far from being a theoretical question, an increasing number of people are questioning the commandment to "honour" father or mother because of childhood horrors rising to the surface. It is no simple matter to forgive past mistreatment. In these circumstances, the bible's admonition to give homage to parents seems to be making a mockery of some very hurtful memories. Sexual abuse cannot be dismissed so easily, but what about the commandment?

When we turn to the bible for assistance, we are faced with a very tricky task. We cannot always lift out a commandment and plunk it down in our culture and expect it to speak to our current problems. In many cases, we have to perform what I call "trans-creation." It's a two-step task. First, one strives to understand the ancient idea with all its historical colouring, and second, create that same idea using our own social standards. Let's apply that method here.

What is the essential message behind the commandment to "honour your father and mother"? As with other biblical rules, it is essential that we understand the context in which such an imperative was formulated. The ten commandments were written in a highly structured and hierarchical society, and it was to that world that they spoke. Men had legal status while women did not. Children were literally nobodies until they reached the age of maturity. Fathers and, by extension, mothers were the cornerstones of that tribal society. It was mandatory that people follow and respect the father of the household, since one's life and livelihood were linked directly to the health and success of the family's head. There was no appreciation for the "freedom of the individual," a principle which reigns supreme in our North American context. Consequently, a child's religious and social duty was to trust and follow the father—no matter how crazy his behaviour might be. This is why Isaac makes no protest when his dad, Abraham, proposes to sacrifice him to God (II Kings 3:27).

A father had complete control over children; they were considered to be his property. He could sell his daughters into slavery (Ex. 21:7) or destroy members of his family if they persuaded him to break faith with God (Deut. 13:6-10). He also gave protection and love to all who came under his control, but he had the final word on all the affairs of the clan. To disobey this all-powerful figure was more like high treason than childhood disobedience.

The fifth commandment was written with a clear and fundamental principle in mind: You were required never to dishonour your parents because in their honour rested the welfare of the entire community. To bring shame upon the father was the ultimate sin, tantamount to undermining the whole family.

In a word, communal and family stability are the principles behind the Holy Scriptures' commandment to honour father and mother. Even the biblically illiterate can see that the values which surrounded the ancient Hebraic family were vastly different from our own. The modern family is held together by a form of romantic attachment between a parental unit and a few children. We place a greater value on love than honour. Children are protected from the excesses of parents by rules which establish the rights of the child—even against a father figure.

To trans-create "honour your father and mother" from the fifth century B.C.E. Hebrew world into twentieth century vocabulary, we might say something like: "protect your family integrity." In our context, that certainly means not just the rights of parents but also the rights of children. In this fashion, we could argue that the commandment is as equally binding on parents as it is on children. Neither has greater privilege, and each is deserving of honour.

Parents who abuse their children break that honour and, therefore, transgress the fifth commandment. Hence, children who cannot forgive their father or mother because of childhood trauma are not sinful.

ARE THERE TRADITIONAL FAMILY VALUES IN THE BIBLE?

In an age when the two-parent family is disinte-grating and divorce rates are skyrocketing, what does Holy Scripture tell us about lasting relationships? Is it natural for so many children to be living with a wide variety of live-in adults? Is our society leaving behind the family values preached in the "good book"?

With troubled hearts, we come to these sacred texts. But before they can shed any light on our dilemma, we must understand two problems.

First, we often have difficulty hearing the bible clearly because we think we already know what it will say. A famous Hebrew scholar once argued that when you open the scriptures, you must know what you see rather than see what you know. That sounds like a bit of sophistry, an overly clever riddle, but this sage was entirely correct. Too many people turn the pages of the scriptures assuming that they will read what they already believe, rather than being confronted with what is actually written.

Here's an example to illustrate how strongly our assumptions influence our reading of the bible. According to Matthew's nativity story, where is Jesus born? The obvious answer jumps to mind. Everyone knows that Jesus was born in a manger, in a cow stall in the shed behind the inn where "there was no room." An easy answer, but entirely misguided by our Sunday School indoctrination. Matthew actually makes no mention of a manger, and seems to imply that Jesus was born in a normal fashion in an established family house. So, whenever we ask what the bible says about any subject, we are faced with a tremendous task—trying to hold back the ingrained stories of our childhood long enough so that the actual text can speak.

Second, the bible is not an encyclopaedia listing facts in neat alphabetical order. We can't look up "family" and find a series of injunctions about its healthy functioning. The bible is fundamentally about an encounter with a living, loving God. The Hebrew and Christian scriptures are not really interested in virtuous concepts or lasting rules. These are secondary to the primary purpose which is to proclaim the goodness and graciousness of the Creator of the Universe who can't resist being involved in human life. All the codes and commandments of the bible are a derivative of the testimony to this first encounter. So our questions, even the burning ones, are not always answered directly. Often, as is the case with the family, we are required to nibble at the edges of the bible's primary focus in order to get food for thought.

That much said, can the bible give us guidance about how to structure family life in this age when there seem to be no lasting principles upon which to build? I think there are three general responses which the scriptures offer us.

First, the biblical picture of the family is biased towards a patriarchal model in which legal and economic power rested with males. While women and widows were protected by certain laws, according to the Hebrew and

Christian scriptures, they were essentially owned by their male associates. Inasmuch as our society has protected the autonomous rights of women, the details of biblical codes concerning family life are, therefore, largely incomprehensible or irrelevant.

Second, the Christian scriptures have an exasperatingly low opinion of family life. Jesus suggests several times that his real family consists of those who are his disciples. He dismisses his mother from his fellowship and treats her without regard even when they are together. The letters of Paul seem to carry on with this rather jaundiced opinion of family by arguing that marriage is a lesser state of existence, second to celibacy.

The romantically founded pattern of a two-parent family with children is a relatively recent invention of the western world. In the time of Jesus, the family was a political and economic unit designed to protect the next of kin from outsiders. The Jesus movement was a direct attack on this clannishness, expanding the idea of family protection to encompass the lost and powerless. A revolutionary idea—even today.

Finally, the bible provides no standard family pattern which fits all contexts. In the Hebrew scriptures, there are many possibilities, all presented as "normal." In certain places, men had many wives (King David for instance). In other cases, men had children by slaves (Abraham had a son by Hagar). On the Christian side, Paul argues that people should make their worshipping community their family, while Jesus himself was born into an adoptive family (Joseph was his stepfather).

Even though there is no model family, the bible offers some basic building blocks which might be useful, no matter the version of family in vogue. Respect and honour seem to be paramount. Love is not always possible, but it seems that the God of the bible yearns for at least an atmosphere of justice and tolerance to reign. After all, we are the keepers of our brothers and sisters, our fathers and mothers. Whatever your family, blended, broken or bent, the bible argues it must be just and life-giving.

The close ties of family are often used by biblical writers as a metaphor for God's relationship to us. It is, therefore, a cherished, central image for the believer. But we must be careful not to be distracted by the "who" of family. The bible isn't so much concerned about who is part of the family as the "what" of the dynamics of family life. It places a high priority on faithfulness, compassion and trust. Where these elements exists, there family is found.

ABORTION AND THE BIBLE

No matter how often or how skillfully you ask the wrong question, you're not going to get the right answer. This has been one of the confusing factors which has muddied the debate when pro-choice or pro-life protagonists have turned to the bible for guidance about abortion. We've been asking it questions which send us down blind alleys, searching with the best of intentions for the right answers, but in the wrong places.

Both sides concede that the bible never mentions abortion specifically, nor does it allude to any practices which might be construed as the termination of fetal life. This is quite surprising, since abortion was practised in the ancient Mediterranean community and was a well-known solution to overpopulation and unwanted pregnancies. Given the scriptures' encyclopaedic coverage of most of life's circumstances, its silence over abortion is both intriguing and frustrating.

What is the right question? Where do we begin to engage the bible so that it will offer guidance in a very thorny issue? Do we ask when life begins? The bible is not entirely clear on this point, but the weight of evidence points to an understanding of human life beginning at conception. But does that help us at all? Do we ask about taking human life? While the bible does argue often for the protection of powerless individuals, there are instances when God sanctions the taking of human life, even innocent lives. For example, God orders Saul to annihilate the Amalekites, an entire people! 1 Samuel 15:3 reads: "Now go and attack Amalek and utterly destroy all they have; do not spare them, but kill both man and woman, child and infant."

What if we were to ask about decision-making and begin the abortion debate from another angle entirely? Does the bible trust women to make wise choices about family life and sexuality? The Book of Proverbs is quite eloquent in its praise of women whose careful household management is life-giving and liberating (Proverbs 31:10-31). Even with its patriarchal framework, the Holy Scriptures acknowledge the power and right of women to step outside expected social and religious norms for the sake of a greater good.

There are several examples of wise and courageous women who work to take exceptional measures to preserve God's peace on earth. But I would turn our attention to the genealogy of Jesus as recorded by the gospel of Matthew 1:1-17 in which only five women are mentioned as ancestors of the one whom Christians call Saviour and Lord. All five, Tamar, Rahab, Ruth, Bathsheba and Mary are extraordinary women. Tamar slept with her father-in-law Judah and became pregnant by him in order to assert her claim for the protection he was bound by law to give her, but which he had previously refused to grant. Rahab, a Canaanite prostitute, was named the "mother" of the nation Israel by helping Joshua's scouts hide in her brothel and avoid capture by the authorities in Jericho. Ruth seduced Boaz and secured a place for herself and Naomi within the chosen people. Bathsheba was forced to submit to David, in what by any other name would be called a rape, and yet later gave birth to Solomon, a great leader of the people. Mary was pregnant out of wedlock, a precarious and quite unrighteous condition.

The author of Matthew grouped these women together, explicitly choosing those females who were wise enough to survive scandalous circumstances because they lived by a higher righteousness than that laid out by common sense or spiritual authority. In this instance, the biblical record does not measure a woman according to a sexual code or because of her conformity to a religious law.

The bible praises women who make wise choices, even in difficult and ambiguous circumstances. Would this principle not guide us in the abortion debate? All too frequently, the ruling religious leaders, often men, have acted as super-parents to women caught with unwanted pregnancies, assuming that they have no authority by which to come to wise decisions of their own making. Taking a leaf from Matthew's gospel, we might well begin the exploration of the question of abortion by trusting mothers to know what to do in life's most difficult moments.

Of course, this approach does not answer all the finer points of abortion, but I believe it begins the debate in a more suitable place. We're closer to asking the right biblical question, for it places women at the centre of a problem which touches their lives most directly, while at the same time inviting men to keep silence and respect the wisdom of women to outline what further questions need to be explored.

WHO REALLY KILLED JESUS?

Who really crucified Jesus? There are some historical problems which are irrelevant to faith, but the question of who was responsible for the cross is one which Christians cannot avoid. On the basis of the misguided assumption that the Jews were responsible for the death of the Christian messiah, Christ-believers through the centuries have massacred Jews. Anti-semitic crowds in far off-Russia and Good Friday rallies in Canada have been whipped into a frenzy through the accusations that the Jews were "Christ-killers."

If we are wise, Christians will approach this question with a very sensitive eye to the damages of Christian anti-Judaism. Recognizing that the four gospel accounts of the crucifixion were written by Jesus-believers, it is important to accept that these early writers were reporting the events of Jesus' final days in a way that supported their burgeoning Christian sect. Consequently, it is not a simple task to uncover who actually executed the carpenter of Galilee.

The first step is to recognize that we may consciously or unconsciously be looking for a "Christian" answer to our question—one which fits with the doctrines we have developed over the years. If we put the brakes on our Christian imaginations and see the situation as clearly as possible, the most obvious answer to our question is that Jesus was crucified by the Romans, probably with very little fuss. No questions, no trial. The Jewish authorities, on the other hand, did not use crucifixion as a method of capital punishment. They left that to the Roman authorities who used the cross as a crowd-control technique.

As more and more archaeological research is undertaken, we recognize that political strife in the time of Jesus was no different than our own. Social systems operated with the same banality and cruelty as those in our own era. Jesus and his disciples lived in an occupied territory, suffered the abuses and excesses that any foreign army might inflict on the local population. We know that the Romans governed with ruthless efficiency, and a human life was taken with a minimum of ceremony. But knowing that the Romans did the deed doesn't answer the question entirely. We have to know what Jesus did to get himself in trouble.

More than likely, Jesus' attack on the temple was one of the chief reasons for his execution. Obviously, he had been confronting the temple authorities for some time, claiming he would destroy what they were about. It is essential to see Jesus' opposition as an entirely Jewish act. If the temple was perceived to be an agent in collusion with Roman tyrants, then an attack on the temple was not only rebellious, but entirely faithful by Jewish standards. No matter how you look at it, what Christians call "the cleansing of the temple" was sufficient cause for an execution. And more than likely, Jesus was the victim of pre-arranged procedures between Roman and temple authorities.

We are indulging in the fantasies of Christian anti-Judaism if we assume that Rome was manipulated into allowing Jesus to be killed. Built on the perspective that

Pontius Pilate was indecisive and weak, past theologians have suggested that he was pushed to the crucifixion by Jewish leaders and so he wasn't ultimately responsible for the death of the Christian messiah. Of course, this milque-toast picture of Pilate is a fabrication. He was anything but helpless. In fact, he was recalled to Rome because of his gratuitous misuse of force—quite an accusation in that tyrannical world.

Jesus was killed by bureaucracy and the interests of power brokers who wanted to suppress the people's yearning for freedom. In that respect, it is possible to say that Jesus is still being crucified today and for exactly the same reasons.

A DAY OF REST

The battle for a constitution-ally protected "day of rest" was lost several years ago. Under the pressure of a secular world view, the designated weekly holiday when all stores closed lost credibility. In our current consumer-driven world, every mall, shopping concourse and strip mall stays open from Monday to Monday—no break in the hours of business. Whenever the urge strikes, you can play the buying game.

Given our "enlightened" and thoroughly modern out-look, we argued that it was unjust, perhaps prejudicial, to allow one religious festival to corrupt or inhibit the urges of our multiethnic population. In this pluralistic age, it makes no sense to highlight the practices of Christians, while ignoring the preferences of other traditions—the Sabbath day of Judaism which is celebrated on Saturday for example. Better to have no special "day of rest."

Like many, I believed that argument. I was ready to sacrifice my childhood habits of Sunday abstinence for the sake of an unbiased society.

No longer! We're wrong not to rest and make it a public policy. We have allowed a rather simplistic piece of logic to cloud our thinking. It may well be that there are some very good social reasons for a designated weekly break for all citizens.

To make these reasons clear, I will have to back up a bit. The Christian practice of a Sunday rest was based on the Jewish observance of the "Sabbath." Declared a commandment, God directs the chosen ones to hallow a special day, keeping it as a holy rest. The Almighty gives several reasons for this practice.

First, when we cease our labours, we imitate the Creator of the Universe. The book of Exodus declares that, "For in six days God made the heavens and the earth and sea and all that these contain, but on the seventh day God rested." Even if the mythology is foreign to us, the basic argument is valid. Creating, any form of creating, whether it's in an office, kitchen or factory, is enhanced when we take a break. We all need regeneration. The earth takes a "Sabbath" that we call winter. Without such pause, all growth would be impossible. Why not human beings?

Moreover, there's an ecological statement being made when we put down our tools. In the day of rest, we are declaring that the earth, our lives and relationships are not defined solely by business. There is more to life than "making" or "achieving." Human existence has a sacred dimension that can only be honoured through respectful pauses in our daily routine. So in this weekly holiday, we reflect the image of our Creator when we suspend all economic activity and gainful employment. Therefore, the Sabbath day is a time when distinctions of money and status are ignored.

That brings us to the second reason which the bible offers for a Sabbath day. In the book of Deuteronomy, the same commandment is based on the need for justice. "Remember you were once a slave in Egypt, and that God brought you out of there with mighty hand and outstretched arm." You get a day off because the Lord of All has liberated slaves from their forced labour. It's only just. Unceasing enslavement to a calculator, lift truck or computer console is sinful, a reduction of our human potential and a very suspect ethical policy.

So let's hear it for the establishment of a true "Sabbath." A day when no one works, no shops are open, no factories running, when families are free to explore the delights of creation at their leisure.

It doesn't matter what day is chosen, and it doesn't necessarily have to come every seven days. There is one last word on the day of rest. A Hebrew scholar once suggested that "Sabbath" might be translated as a term which denoted "enough." It was a day and a dream which declared that enough is enough. We have no need for excess. Essentially, it contains a vision of how the world might be—a place where no one takes more than their share and all people have what belongs rightfully to them.

Sabbath—a glorious day indeed!

DOES THE BIBLE CONDEMN HOMOSEXUALITY?

The bible can be like a mirror, reflecting back whatever is projected into it. For instance, if you go to the bible to find justification for the male power which keeps women in their place, you can turn to Paul's letter to the church in Corinth (1 Corinthians 14:34-35) and find that for which you're looking. Or, if you want the scriptures to bolster your claim that private property is evil, just open the gospel of Matthew 6:19. If we go to the bible determined to uncover a supporting proof for our particular hobby horse, we'll find it.

Therefore, in an honest approach to the scriptures, the challenge is to suspend our preconceived biases and recognize when we may be reading into the text what isn't actually there. There are many instances where the words of the bible may seem similar to our own, but the underlying cultural and social assumptions are radically different. The bible's attitude to homosexuality is a case in which the "good book" doesn't always mean what we think.

Some people turn immediately to the Sodom and Gomorrah story as clear evidence for the scriptures' intolerance of homosexual behaviour. If we read the story without prior assumptions, we will see that it is not about same-sex sexual intercourse, but gang rape. The abomination of the Sodomites was not their desire to interact romantically with other men. The story in Genesis 19 portrays the Sodomites as angry men who want to humiliate and subjugate the strangers that have entered their city. There is every reason to believe these men were heterosexuals who wanted to employ anal intercourse as an act of violation. Hence, as a story, it doesn't help us at all in determining the bible's attitude to homosexuality.

We can turn to Leviticus 18:22 or 20:13, two verses which are essentially identical, condemning men being with other men, but, again, we may be fooled. It is important to note that the Hebrew language does not have a word for homosexual or homosexuality. The actual wording in the verses in question is: "A man shall not lie down with another man with the lyings of a woman." Can anyone in our age understand what these ancient writers meant by "the lyings of a woman"? Were the Hebrews opposed to anal intercourse, the fact that a man might take the woman's role or the idea of two men sleeping with each other? Because of these questions, I believe Leviticus does more to confuse our understanding of the bible's attitude to homosexuality than enlighten it.

All the texts in the Hebrew scriptures which allude to

homosexual behaviour are gender-specific, referring only to men. There is no mention of women wanting the company of other women or lesbian orientation, and I have no idea what that silence might mean. Moreover, there is no appreciation of the distinction between act and orientation.

In the Christian scriptures, there are three passages which touch on homosexuality. Two of the three mention it in a list of vices which the early Christian church found abhorrent. Are all the items on the list of equal weight—is gossiping and drunkenness of equal repugnance as homosexual prostitution (1 Timothy 1:8-11, 1 Corinthians 6:9-11)? Some scholars suggest that in both Corinthians and Timothy, the list is a generic formulation with no special weight given to any one specific item. Others maintain that the terms referring to homosexual behaviour found in these two lists are, in fact, the technical terms used to describe the buying and selling of sexual gratification and the underlying problem was this mercantile distortion of God's gift of sexuality.

The final and only passage in the bible which alludes to what we might recognize as a homosexual encounter between consenting partners is found in Paul's letter to the church in Rome (Romans 1:26). Clearly, the apostle is vexed over what he considers to be unnatural behaviour. Men and women were leaving what he considered to be the "norm" and falling into perverse actions. It should be noted that the same author thought it was contrary to accepted principles for women to speak in church (1 Corinthians 14: 34-35) and had no qualms about the normality of human beings being owned as slaves (Philemon 1:15-16). I find it curious that most Christians don't listen to Paul's definition of the "natural order" in these two instances but accept his sexual pronouncements word for word.

In total, the bible contains six phrases which touch on homosexual behaviour. Given the hundreds of commandments and thousands of pages, I can't see how homosexuality is of much interest to the scriptures. The bible contains much more material condoning slavery and confining the rights of women than it does speaking about homosexuality. The fact that many Christians condemn homosexuality with righteous appeals to the scriptures is an example of bringing to the bible what is really a twentieth century preoccupation and pretending that a handful of sentences from scripture correspond to our modern anxieties over sexuality.

The best response that scripture can give with regard to homosexuality is the declaration that our Creator is very often not concerned about the "who" of relationship so much as the "how." It simply asks if the relationship is functioning according to principles of justice and dignity? Does the partnership demonstrate mutual trust and compassion? If so, it is blessed by God.

DIVORCE, BIBLICAL STYLE

Divorce hurts. When parents separate, there are a number of pains compounded by the hardships of dissolved relationship. Children are often split off from mother or father or grandparents, lifelong conversations between in-laws are cut short and communication becomes hard-edged for everyone.

I may be dismayed by the bible's mystery, but it is certainly an honest book when it speaks of romance and relationships. It maintains that human beings are, by their very nature, lovers, and it is precisely our capacity to love which gets us into trouble, causing pain and betrayal. It may not be what we want—an indexed guide to life's pitfalls, but the bible doesn't sugar-coat the trials of marriage.

While mature conjugal respect and faithfulness are extolled as virtues in the "good book," it recognizes marital breakdown as a regrettable possibility. Infidelity, jealousy, bitterness and envy happen, and because of its realism, the bible allows for divorce.

Even though humans seek to mate for life, the scriptures are quite clear that human life is a fluid state. We are not fixed beings, predetermined for all time, so we make promises we cannot keep. Hurtful deeds, which once seemed scandalous and beyond our capabilities, are the very things we find ourselves doing. It sounds like a cliche, but the bible does, indeed, argue that "to err is human." Therefore, let the first word of the bible about divorce be "understanding." Divorce is never commended, but the scriptures understand that it is sometimes necessary.

The obvious question arises: Under what circumstances does the bible allow for divorce? Before I answer that question, we need to be reminded that there are at least two thousand years of history separating us from the scriptures' restrictions on divorce. The underlying motivations by which they justify the dissolution of marriage may, in some cases, be irrelevant or even misleading in the present context. The challenge is to interpret the old injunctions and motivations in such a way as they make sense today.

For example, in the bible, divorce was initiated largely by the husband. This should not surprise us, since the culture from which the scriptures originate was patriarchal. Women had no legal status, so were unable to send their husbands away. The underlying assumption of both the Christian and Hebrew scriptures is that the male of the household held all the power and was given considerable latitude, being able to dismiss his wife for such a vague reason as his own "dislike" of her (Deut. 24:3).

Modern sensitivities balk at such an imbalance of matrimonial power. Certain scholars suggest that this was precisely the intent of Jesus. By restricting divorce severely, he was attempting to redress this injustice, making men as accountable to their wives as wives were to their husbands.

While the bible offers several concrete reasons for divorce—childlessness (Malachi 2:15), religious principles (Ezra 1:3,44), and adultery (Duet. 24:1)—behind the various specifics is the Biblical understanding of marriage as a covenant. It is a God-inspired agreement based on faithfulness. Even though the scriptures try to regulate the economic and political side of marriage, a dimension still very present today, it maintains that the covenant of marriage is held together by faith rather than by legal contracts. When faith is broken, so is the marriage (Malachi 2:13-17). It is interesting to note that faithlessness is the only condition under which Jesus allows for divorce (Mat. 5:32).

Faith is broken in many ways. Sexual infidelity can be one way to break faith, and it was as potent a problem in biblical times as it is in our own, though for different reasons. The scriptures view adultery largely as a property issue. This was certainly the case in the adultery of King David in 2 Samuel 1-10, while our present culture views it as a question of trust.

Faith is also broken through violence or abuse. This seems to be a preoccupation of the prophet Malachi who declares that God hates the cruelty which breaks the original covenant of marriage (Mal. 2:16). Lamenting the loss of peace, respect and unity of purpose, God calls people to a relationship based on justice and trust. When mutual faith is broken through destructive behaviour, the marriage covenant ceases to be binding.

The bible is honest enough to lament divorce. It is never a happy occurrence, but the scriptures recognize that it may be the only way to re-establish healthy human relationships.

WHO'S THE BAD GUY?

"Eeeny, meenie, mynie, moe..." That's how the school yard chant began. Calling up teams for everything from Marvel Marbles to British Bulldog, we used that time-tested chant to eliminate one player after another. Those sent from the circle were the bad guys, while the ones who remained were the good guys.

Whether one was left inside or banished, there was something satisfying about that selection process. There were no doubts, no troubling ambiguities. The lines were clearly drawn.

As we approach the turn of the millennium, many folk are troubled by what seems to be a lack of clarity about who is or is not responsible for what appears to be a steady decline in our social order. Why can't we point out the bad guys any more?

Our uncertainty produces an apocalyptic anxiety—the desperation to sort it all out before it's too late. Believers, quite naturally, turn to their sacred writings in search of reassurance. Surely, if we study the bible predictions with an Agatha Christie watchfulness, we will uncover the secret code or devious designs of the anti-Christ. Who doesn't want to find the end-of-the-age plot line and finally have someone on whom to pin the disintegration of our culture?

In the mythic scenes of the Book of Daniel, we unravel what we think is an ancient puzzle pointing to a world conspiracy overwhelming the moral society. With the beginning of another thousand year cycle looming large, fundamentalists of all stripes comb through the book of Revelation, lifting out a complicated scenario of increasing catastrophes orchestrated by the anti-Christ.

In every age, believers have sensed there is a force for evil working in the world and have, consequently, constructed elaborate explanations. Over the centuries, everyone has had their turn being the "bad guy." Scholars and fanatics have variously argued that the bible revealed a world conspiracy of anarchist bankers or communist atheists. Popes, monarchs and Jews have been the most favoured targets of this finger pointing. Gays, blacks, women, the peasant and the poor all become easy pickings for our fear—send them away. Demonize them and reject them.

Of course, it would be terribly reassuring if, as in our schoolyard games, we could single out the villain, the devilish entanglements of destruction. But, no matter how tempting the year 2000 may appear to spiritualists and millenialists alike, the bible does not lend itself to this variety of detective work and naturally resists simplistic answers. It was not written by a single hand, and if you read it backwards or upside down you will not discover a "secret" mystery. While it may be entertaining, it is pointless to regard the scriptures like a puzzle waiting to be solved by the most recent version of enlightenment.

On the question of evil, the bible is very clear. If there is a villain, a devil, or devilish plot behind our corruption as a civilization, it is us. According to the "old, old story," people create much of their own misery by pretending to be something they aren't. Through lust for power or cowardice in purpose, human beings ensnare themselves.

The biblical Creator did not program the earth with a self-destruct code written into its genes. On the contrary. The scriptures' predominant message, one repeated from the Rainbow Covenant with Noah to the vision of a new earth in Jerusalem, is that God longs for the earth's wholeness and health.

So at the risk of sounding rather anti-climatic, I suggest we approach the end of the millennium not as if each day were our last, but rather as if we are going to live forever. In that case, we will quite naturally cease our paranoid "we-they" antics designed to blame the "bad" people for our present state and play a game where everyone is on the same side.

3 OUT OF THE MOUTHS OF BABES

LET'S DANCE

"I BE TWO! I BE TWO!" That's what little Maude shouted as she waltzed about the dining room on her second birthday. A whirling smile, waving her arms in all directions, she's caught up in a flash of ecstasy.

What a wonderful surprise, a day of exaltation! Yesterday, she was only one (a lowly and insignificant age when viewed from the dizzy heights of older toddlerhood), and today she is two—a mature and proper age, one of which to be proud. And it all happens without any effort, you just wait long enough and bingo! You're one year older.

In this one instant of joy, all else is blotted out. Who cares if the baseball pennant race is starting? Ask Maude if she notices the wind blowing the new falling snow. Does she wring her hands, worrying that the premier is going to chop more social programs? Ask her if she is even aware that the Edmonton Eskimos are still short of their goal for season tickets. Not even the prospect of a holiday in the mountains could turn her mind from the sheer joy of this day.

I BE TWO! Surprise triumphs over all else. What happened to surprise—that heart-stopping, mind-fogging exhilaration of a child? Have we lost it? In our earnest desire to grow up and become responsible adults, have we mislaid the capacity to be surprised by life? To dance when the heartbeat of creation breaks into our daily routine? I think so.

What a shame, that life holds no surprises any more.

Look at us. We struggle out of bed in the morning,

groaning our way through breakfast. Then into the car, hands grasped tightly on the wheel, trying to clear the mist from our eyes. Who has time to stop and be surprised? We have to get to work. Once at our desk, there are messages to return, voice mail to answer, letters to write. Who has the energy for surprises when there's a heavy luncheon date with a client and a whole afternoon full of meetings.

Boring!—that's us. It's built into the North American lifestyle. After we hit thirty, we imagine that this is the way it must be, should be. There are no hidden treasures buried beneath our daily routine, no "Ah Ha" moments lurking around the next corner, just drudgery. Get up, work, eat, sleep—maybe some sex in there, but even that is all too predictable.

Life is empty; that's the sign we should hang over the latter part of the twentieth century. As adults we have settled into a comfortable, emotional coma, no longer able to feel surprise, not over ethnic cleansing or suburban mass murders. In our cynical and lazy way we mumble, "There's nothing new under the sun."

I want to shout and scream: "No, don't do it. Don't fall into the apathy trap where surprise is stifled and joy is strangled, where the dance is stilled."

But, we are now adults. The dance is stilled because we have some very harsh question to confront. The death of a loved one, the despair of the unemployed, the despondency of our teenagers. Our existence is not easy, and it may seem frivolous or lighthearted to consider dancing when the times seem so hard. Aren't we being a bit unfeeling when injustice and brokenness are so prevalent? It's hard to dance and appreciate the surprises of life, when one is faced with the blinding lights of oncoming problems.

If you feel like giving up on life's surprises, take emergency measures, NOW! Stop what you're doing and watch a young child at play. See how everything is new—the colour of toothpaste, flowers in the vase on the window ledge, a dog's furry coat. It's all fresh and alive and surprising! Go ahead take the time—even if you don't have a young child to guide you. Think back and remember . . . Imagine it's the fall of the year. Do you recall the rich, musty fragrance of dry leaves? Conjures up the haunting mystery of Halloween, doesn't it? A shadowy darkness when nothing is as it seems. Surprises? Why there's a whole treat bag full of them on that night. How about the fall suppers; crowds of adults and children jostling to find a place, church tables bending under the strain of steaming dishes all designed to make your mouth water. How many pieces of pie did you have? Six, seven? My brother once ate ten, grinning from ear to ear. Surprise? I was awestruck at such an accomplishment. Who can forget the whiff of snow in the air; catching you unaware as if fall would last forever? Surprises? They filled and overflowed the vessel our childhood. How sad it is that as we get older we grow calluses over that part of our soul—no longer feeling the rub of surprise—at least not without a considerable amount of work.

But all is not lost. Like many things in life, your surprise ability can be relearned. Even if you've forgotten the steps, you can relearn the dance. It begins with a deep breath. Relax a bit. Catch of whiff of what's in the air. Open your eyes. Wonder is waiting for you—in the touch of a tiny hand, in the icicle swaying off a spruce in the crisp winter air, in the liberating laughter of small children. Try it! Get out there and exercise your surprise muscles.

Then join with Maude, dance about the kitchen. Dare to be foolish and shout, "I BE TWO!"

HEAD TO HEART: THE PRIMAL POSITION OF LOVING

Hannah came for a visit last week. What a blessing! All of 15 months old, she has a smile that can charm a cookie out of the meanest spirit and a curiosity that travels about the kitchen with lightning speed.

Apart from the joy of her company, Hannah awakened in me a gift that has been dormant, almost forgotten. She elicited from me a care-giving skill, much appreciated by parents everywhere but rarely studied as a field of research: putting babies to sleep. Helping an infant to give in to their tiredness and rest their roving eyes is not a spectacular sport. It wouldn't draw crowds, but I am good at it. In fact, if it was ever declared an Olympic event, I think I would qualify for the national team.

Hannah was fussing a bit, the I-want-sleep-but-I-can't-figure-it-out whimpering. I scooped her up and before she knew what was happening, she was sound asleep. Lest you think this was just luck, it should be noted that I did it twice, the second "putting to sleep" session being required when the ringing of our phone woke Hannah up in mid-snooze.

What's my technique? Well, it's quite simple, actually. Having long arms and a strong heartbeat, I keep the child's head firmly against my chest and hold her body stable as I rock back and forth on my heels. Five to ten minutes and bingo, she's asleep. With particularly troubled babies, a round or two of Edelweiss combined with a little more vigorous rocking and the desired sleep-state is achieved. I can't say it's my singing that works this miracle, rather I sense it is the heartbeat. After all, babies grew up with that sound ringing in their ears for nine months. What better way to feel calm and relaxed than with the touch and feel of that maternal beating?

Head to heart—the primal position which works on babies, also has a profound influence on all ages. Who doesn't marvel at the sound of a human heart beating? What closer tie is there for lovers?

Besides initiating a discussion on the possibility of baby slumber as a national sport, I am telling you about Hannah because she helped me to recognize the need for all human beings to feel that basic rhythm of loving and living. It's not an option or an extra. It is central to becoming whole and healthy.

In a unique and mysterious fashion, the sound of a

heartbeat takes us home, brings us back to our original state, binds up broken dreams and reminds us what life is all about. In its never ceasing rhythm, we feel an assurance and closeness and hear the timeless message that we are not alone.

Now, this healing heartbeat pulses in many places besides the human breast. There is a heartbeat in the cycle of the seasons, rhythms written into our summers and winters, life and death, work and rest, action and repose. Our well-being is directly linked to keeping in touch with that ancient pattern. As we gaze upon the birth of spring, we are reminded that the beating rhythms of our individual lives are part of a greater rhythm. The small heartbeats within ourselves are echoes of a greater heartbeat out there.

So, do yourself a favour. Put your head to someone's heart and then offer your heartbeat to another in turn. Who knows, apart from having a greater awareness of our place in the universe, we all might sleep better.

THE GREAT LIE

When did you grow out of childhood and into adolescence? Can you recall an incident, a shining moment which marked the watershed between comfortable innocence and awakening maturity? Was it that first kiss furtively stolen behind a closed door?

Perhaps it was a tragic injury which forced you to face the inequality of life? I can recall the moment when I grew up, and it's a rather telling incident. My father had always locked the garage at night before he retired for the evening. There weren't a lot of thefts in my home town, but it was his habit. At one point, he lost the key and instructed his children in a voice loud and clear, "Don't lock the garage door!" One day, I came home all excited about my school work. Parking my bike in its usual place in the garage, I ran out, and without thinking, shoved the lock into place. Click! I whistled my way from the locked garage trying not to look like the son who had just transgressed his father's commandments, but my guilt followed me like a shadow. As it happened, by fate or providence (I cannot tell which), my father was asked to preside at a funeral that afternoon. To double my sin, I had inadvertently locked his car inside the garage. Imagine his state of mind when, with only a few minutes to spare, he rushed out of the house to find his car inside a barred building—with no hope of a key.

That night, he marched all three children into the living room for an interrogation. I can still see the beige carpet beneath my scuffed black runners. Shame had me looking down a lot. Dad went from child to child. "Did you lock the garage door?" My sister said, "No!" She could sound so injured by false accusations. My brother also said, "No," but he was more puzzled than hurt. Dad turned to me. "Did you lock the garage door?" I said, "No." It was a sheepish ploy, and I expected the heavens to open up and a lightning bolt to strike me dead.

Nothing happened! My father stalked off under a cloud. And to my child's mind, lying had worked. I told a falsehood and was saved. At that moment, I left childhood and discovered the ambiguity and mixed emotions of an adult existence. I was happy to be rescued from punishment but also vexed and disappointed that deception was so easily overlooked.

Is it not true that our culture has also followed this pattern, shifting from one stage of its life to another by lying about its actions? Have we not moved from a time of relative social compassion into a season of social disregard and fiscal mean-spiritedness by lying to ourselves? We have lied about the pain and suffering incurred by closing hospitals, downsizing government services, restraining cultural institutions, and cutting social safety nets. We have pretended that the only economic priority for this decade is attacking the deficit and reducing the debt, while systematically disregarding the financial burdens which the destitute must now bear.

At its root, lying is sin. I didn't know that as a child, but as I mature, I recognize that every falsehood chips away at the integrity of my soul. When we lie, we break faith with an inherent justice of human living. Either we pretend we are more important than we really are, putting ourselves and our own interests above the claims of truth, or we pretend we are less than we are, avoiding the natural responsibilities of human existence. Either way, our lying is a corrosive agent for the soul.

Lying is also addictive. Little white lies seem innocent enough, but the danger grows when we allow them to pile up. It becomes a way of living, and eventually we begin to believe our own untruths, inaccuracies, skewed ideas and the many mini-falsehoods we hold up to trick other people. In the final analysis, we hurt ourselves through lying by diminishing our own sense of self worth and disregarding what is and what could be. Reality becomes indistinguishable from fantasy.

When we as a people begin to lie to ourselves, we are in deep trouble. We lose touch with our soul and forget the spirit that binds us together. Our young people grow disheartened and jaded, while the marginalized become even more cynical.

It is precisely that danger of collective lying which I see lurking behind the upbeat pronouncements about our economic growth, the bright future that lies ahead and the opportunities for bold new financial initiatives.

Our health as a people begins when we acknowledge life as it really is, recognizing all the ramifications of our actions. It's time to stop the lie and start naming the victims of our austerity measures. Who are the people that suffer most when the safety nets are cut loose, or when the farm is lost? Let's at least be honest about the pain caused by the shifting sands of global economics.

Just as lying marked the transition from childhood to adolescence for me, our maturity as a people begins when we let go of lying and learn truth-telling as a way of being.

FOREVER YOUNG: THE VIRTUE OF PLAY

I met Peter Pan last Saturday — above the 60th parallel in Yellowknife of all places. While going round the circle of young faces at a weekend retreat, each reciting their name—Tim, Elizabeth, Abby, Gary, Heather—who should be present but Peter Pan. I had no idea he flew so far north, but there was no mistaking the I'm-made-for- play smile and that tomboyish defiance. No question about it. This was Peter Pan and he was a she! Her other name was Kieran, and she would answer to that if necessary, but it was clear that Peter Pan was her preference. For two days I tested her, and each time I asked who she was, she firmly and seriously replied, "Peter Pan."

There is something quite daunting about a child's imagination. Call it an endless capacity for credulity, an effortless suspension of rational cognition, or simply an illusory escape, it is awe-inspiring to behold. This young five-year-old could touch another dimension. Momentarily leaving behind the troublesome spelling lessons and the Sunday-school moralisms, she flies off to Neverland where you don't have to grow up. In that altered space, as we all know, heroines and pirates clash, an evil crocodile lies in wait for even more sinister Captain Hook, and costumed shadows dance about the campfires on the hill. Once having arrived in this land of endless play, time stands still and all aging or decay is left behind. Magnificent! So what's the matter with the rest of us who live down here on earth? Did we really achieve that much when we became adults? Was the rush hour traffic that alluring? How about the not-to-be-missed political wrangling that colours all mature institutions from the curling rink to the family funeral? Did we leave our childhood behind so that we could be plagued by those headaches of adulthood? Perhaps it was the banality of adult entertainment that enticed us to abandon our childish ways—the mindless round of Friday night beer-parlour parties, and the Thursday evening vegging-out-in-front-of-the-TV tedium.

Was it really wise to grow up? Do you ever wake up in a cold sweat wondering if it was all worth it? You've just had that recurring nightmare—on-the-treadmill-not-quite-making-it variety in which you know you are a failure as an adult. In mine, I'm always scribbling notes to a very important speech while walking up to the podium and my grade two teacher, Miss Lewis, is sitting in the front row scolding, "You'll never amount to much." So who needs maturity anyway? It's in the nighttime of our fears that we ask if we actually gained that much when we grew up. Perhaps Peter Pan was right! Maybe the never-setting sun-shine of childhood has some salutary dimensions that we missed in our mad dash to get ahead, get a job, and get respectable.

What does Peter Pan know that we have forgotten? Isn't his unique genius evident in his playful attitude? For Pan, the Lost Boys, Tinkerbell, Nancy, Michael and even Captain Hook, play is as important as work. In that enchanted world, there is continual amusement, and while that may seem like an overly rich diet, the fable reminds us of the centrality of play within a healthy existence. Our lives are not to be sweated from birth until life closes. The Creator of all gave us a magnificent world to enjoy. Why ignore it? Play is a vehicle for expressing and sharing our deep satisfaction over bodily existence. Ask yourself if, on your deathbed, you will wish that you had spent more time at the office, on the shop floor or kitchen sink.

I rest my case. Healthy play is the spice and spirit which makes the whole shooting match worth enduring. Moreover, play is a way to test ourselves against the sharp edges of living while they still have safety guards. A glance at the story gives ample evidence of that fact. Through their play, the characters explore the meaning of greed, the question of courage, and the mystery of immortality, to name only a few issues. All the profound quandaries of life are present in their playacting. As children and adults, we test our limits and our potential through play.

Finally, while playing we commune with the child within, the whimsical, trusting being who feeds our imagination and vision, who asks why the world can't be better, more loving and trustworthy, and who waters the garden of our hopes. Without that child we die, and without play we'll never meet that wise inner being.

Thank you Peter Pan (a.k.a. Kieran) for you have reminded us that inside we are still children, that there is a delightful, delicious world of expectations and dreams which enriches all life and which is as close as the twinkling of an eye.

SALVATION IS A DIRTY WORD

Do you know what "succedaneous" means? Neither did I until Harley, my five-year-old friend, used it in a sentence recently. He learned it (along with other mouth size words like "apocalyptic" and "eschatology") from his mother who was once a dental hygienist. The term refers to the sequence in which teeth grow in the mouth. "Baby" teeth, as they are called, will come in, fall out and be replaced in a succedaneous pattern, one rank replacing the next.

It's nice to know what a big word means, but why not just be clear. If you're sitting in the dentist's chair wouldn't it make you feel more at ease to know your dentures are coming in the correct sequence rather than "succedaneously"?

Jargon can certainly get in the way, and there's nothing like the fog factor in religious lingo to confuse the mind. Here's another "S" word that is often misunderstood. "Salvation." What does it mean and how can we understand it in this secular society?

I suspect that many believers live by the assumption that salvation is something that happens in heaven. We have to wait until we are dead and buried. Then God will open up a celestial ledger, tally up our faults and our good deeds, and grant us either heavenly rest or eternal damnation.

While I wouldn't want to deny that salvation is a spiritual matter, it distresses me that it has never been appreciated as an earthly, physical affair. Our eyes naturally drift skyward, but what if our salvation were to be found right under our noses.

Here's an example. There was a man who had two adopted daughters. Before they arrived at his doorstep without parent or guardian, they had suffered much abuse and had tasted more than a lifetime's worth of agony. Consequently, they transferred some of their grief to the adopted father. In fact, as they grew, he was the brunt of a good deal of anger coming from their troubled souls. You can't blame the girls, and you can't blame the dad, but it was not an easy mixture for anyone.

In her fourteenth year, the oldest girl got into such bad company and caused such a commotion in the home that the family had to let her go out on her own. That's what she wanted. "Let me make my own rules," she said. And she did. It was not a pretty sight. She got into drugs, thought she was pregnant, lost out on school, and spent her evenings chasing after a very cruel and ignorant young man.

For weeks, the family had no idea of her whereabouts, and eventually they imagined she had left town for foreign parts where the bright lights shone. She always wanted to be a model. Maybe she was dead or in jail. No one knew. The stubborn refusal of the daughter to see clearly how her family loved her was matched by the parents' bitterness over their failure to keep her home.

Then, one day there was a phone call from hell. "Please help me! Make me safe again!" The prodigal daughter was coming home ... tonight. The prodigal father was frightened and hesitant when the doorbell rang. In the light of the hall lamp, the scars were visible on his child's face. The father stood equally wounded, though in more invisible ways. Tension was stiff in the air. Finally, after many awkward moments, came the hug, tentative at first, but life-saving in the end.

For this family, salvation was not an other-worldly, after-death experience. Salvation was the phone call. It was the lost daughter walking up to the front door and the lost father opening it.

In many circumstances, salvation is not the Hallelujah chorus version of purity and clarity—a light shining from the heavens. That does happen, but more often than not, it's a dirty word—mixed with all the confusion of earthly existence, with half-baked measures and leftover virtue. God appears in some strange garb at times; it is not always easy to see salvation even when it comes up to our door and knocks.

Like Harley, many of us know the words, but it will take some serious living before we can appreciate their full meaning. And that's okay because God is patient.

THE FUNDAMENTALS OF FAITH

Sometimes we forget the key reasons for being religious. It took Jesse, my three-year-old buddy, to remind me of the central point of my spiritual journey. Why should I be surprised? After all, faith is, at its roots, a child's issue.

We were walking along the lake shore in the sunshine, having just called my home. Jesse had wanted to take the phone first, since my partner is the apple of his eye (after Shanna, the six-year-old goddess who graces his fantasies). Without much thought, I had reclaimed the receiver and ended the conversation with a perfunctory, "I love you."

Jesse walked in silence for a bit, kicking at the sand. Something was weighing on his mind. Looking up at the setting sun, he asked in the unabashed I-really-want-to-know manner only kids under five can muster, "Why do you love her?" He does not yet understand the romantic attachment between adults, nor has he measured the fire of passion for the beating of another heart. At this point, he's just curious about why love happens.

I stopped in my tracks. That's it, isn't it? The chief question of faith. "Why love?" After all the dogmatic principles are pronounced from the pulpit and once the ringing appeals to orthodoxy or fundamentalism are silenced, Jesse's simple question remains: "Why do we love?" The faith story spanning the centuries begins and ends on that sticky point.

So Jesse, here's the answer I fumbled to give you back then on the beach. First, we love because we were made for it. Like a factory-installed feature of human life, we reach out beyond our own selves to touch another. You're closest to your mother, father and brother right now. But as the years pass, you will search for someone who loves you beyond familial obligation. You'll want to love because it just bursts out. There's a mingling of physical ache and spiritual tenderness that cannot be dampened nor ignored. It just is and will not be denied.

Second, you might think of this love as the fixed pattern of the whole of creation. At its core, this need to love arises because we came from love, and all that we do is a journey back to the love that created us in the first place. That may sound a bit trite until you see the love which blossoms and grows through the cycle of the seasons and in the regular beat of life and death. Our human love is a way to fit with the rhythm.

Finally, we love because we seek a concrete expression of that which is hypothetical. In time, you will notice that there is something scandalous about loving, since it is never satisfied with a general principle nor a theoretical possibility. It always seeks embodiment in singularity. You will want to fall in love, not with the whole world but with one person. I'm not trying to say there is only one love for everyone, but love does strive to find an object—an individual. That it fixes itself on a particular being is a mystery beyond our mind's grasp. That's just how it works, and that's why I love her.

Of course, loving is not just about romance between two people. There is also the love of a higher power, the

One who made us. These two loves are not unconnected—faith in God and faith in a specific someone. We can love in the abstract because we also love in the particular. That is the primal religious truth, the one and only commandment—to love.

Jesse, that's the answer to your question. It has taken me a few weeks to come up with a satisfactory response. And along the way, I've discovered why I'm also such a religious person ... just like you. Thanks.

4 SIN BOLDLY

SIN BOLDLY

Religion has become far too "tight" for its own good. Boring. Bland. That's what we believers have become. Sitting in our all too neat and predictable rows, we spend much of our time "witnessing" with half-baked and often timid adorations of the Creator. No emotion — please! What could be a bold declaration of God's blessings has grown to look and feel more like God's funeral. Shame on us! What happened to our "Joy to the World"?

Hester Henchrow taught me that church could be fun. In a brilliant act of bravado, she changed my appreciation of faith-filled living. She was a member of my father's church, and to a young boy of nine, she always appeared to be to a wild rose bursting the bounds of the manicured ecclesiastical garden patch. On Sunday mornings, she would swagger through the lower hall of the church to the choir room in a black cocktail dress, fishnet stockings and a hairdo that would knock your eyes out. Along the way, she hugged everyone in sight—this was long before it became a religious fashion. Not given to whispering, Hester's laughter preceded her wherever she went, changing even the grumpiest face into one of merriment.

One year, Hester was assigned to a rather elderly women's group—an anomaly resulting from the yearly division of the church women into separate working units. (In hindsight, it was providence at work!) Hester's gang was not exactly a sparkling band of zealots. They were rather hesitant souls who looked upon the church as a haven in which to hide from the world's demands. Their gatherings were characterized by neatly sliced cucumber rolls (no crusts) and weekly spoonfuls of sobering devotional moralisms.

It was the practice of the day that each group would take a turn coming to the minister's home for a potluck supper—an "on your best behaviour" event. So over they came one hot summer evening. My mother supplied the punch and tea, and the women brought the food. There were green jellied apologies, dainty little hesitations and a plateful of delicate blushes. It was a respectable religious meal if ever there was one.

Hester was hard at work trying to give the gathering some zing. At first, her jokes garnered just a few titters, but as the evening progressed and the food and drink disappeared, the delicate smiles blossomed into fruity laughter. Close-lipped matrons dished up a host of hilarious stories, each one bringing the gathering closer to hysteria. We could hardly believe the transformation. Women who often looked as uptight as tea cups ready to crack were telling bawdy jokes that broke all the religious barriers.

It was the miracle of shared food and drink that melted their ice so thoroughly. Cheers rose as they swapped recipes. Of special interest was my mother's punch. "Never had anything like it," they said. "Let's serve it at the next general assembly." "How delicious." What a wonderful meeting! If only all church gatherings could be so full of life. For an instant, they forgot their tentative half measures and drank from the fullness of life.

They all filed out of the house in a glow that would not wilt, no matter the heat outside. As she was leaving, Hester took my father aside to tell him of her contribution to the potluck supper. "Victor," she said, "you told us Luther said to 'sin boldly.' Well, I took his advice because it seemed that God needed a little help with this lot. I spiked the punch."

Religion should not be the dry-as-dust practice that it so often becomes. I thank Hester for illustrating how to take the gift of life joyously with both hands and share it lavishly—and that a little "bold sinning" can go a long way!

So, do we need to be asked twice? More punch, indeed!

LIFE IS A GIFT TO BE TESTED

I don't do ice, and I don't do puddles. Can you blame me? After all, I'm plowing through the often troubled, sometimes tranquil waters of middle age. I gave up my playtime boots long ago and now don my business-as-usual toe rubbers when I go out into the elements. I have trouble recalling last night's dinner menu let alone the wild joys of childhood winter thaws. When the temperature rises to melt the winter blanket, I don't think sliding or slush. Utility and security cover the soles of my feet. Alas, you know that age is winning when the minions of adults pray to the powers of heaven, "Take me south for a break."

Thank goodness for our younger friends who drag us away from these hunker-down-and-hole-up retreats from living. The five year old hand that took mine last week was determined, not deterred.

Picture the scene.

It's a lazy Sunday afternoon. Harley and I had just seen the re-issued classic "Star Wars" (a wonderful excuse for the late bloomer generation to escape into an epic which shaped our adolescence). Compared to the dark theatre, the sun was bright. So why not walk home? My companion led the way.

The first sign that this was not going to be your garden variety, adult-like stroll came at the crosswalk. Still holding hands, I was dragging us toward dry ground, but he was pulling steadfastly toward the pools of slush and sand. Allowing him a bit of latitude but hanging on tight, I was confused and then delighted to see that he hit every puddle with an affirmative splot—water everywhere—up my leg, down his boot, sparkles and splutters radiating out in all directions. Silly me. I had forgotten how much fun it was. Let the dry cleaners do their worst—there's nothing like the "rush" of propriety defied.

The street crossing accomplished with real flair, my young buddy looked up, smiling and proud. What better achievement could there be? His grin sparked a flashback reminding me of the spring thaws of my childhood when I would walk out into the middle of large roadside puddles, daring the water to spill over the top of my super-hero boots. It was the ultimate badge of courage.

But the puddles were just the beginning. We turned the corner into my neighbourhood, and several blocks of ice-smeared sidewalks loomed ahead. Appropriate adult admonitions were on the tip on my tongue. "Watch the ice." "Don't run too quickly now." "Be careful."

Obviously, my little friend thought life was too much fun to be careful. "Let's slide," he cried out, and before I could refuse, he was pulling me again. I hadn't done this in years. You remember—the pell-mell canter along the ice and then the slick, flat-footed glide. Once was never enough. Twice was too few. There was always another patch of slideable sidewalk waiting to be tested.

I realize that social wisdom argues for "better safe than sorry," and in many specific instances, this is a good moral to follow. But in the general business of living, many religious traditions will argue that those who risk nothing, gain nothing. If we close our mornings to the unexpected or keep our evenings protected from any surprises, we will lose them. The days we have been allotted by our Creator are a gift to be tested and tried.

While spiritual wisdom rests in finding a healthy balance between taking a chance and seeking security, in the current context of self-centred isolation, maybe we need to emphasize reaching out beyond our self-serving boundaries. A little abandonment and risk-taking is a helpful thing.

So why not join me and my friend—hold on tight and slide! Maybe we should stick "Post-its" to our foreheads as reminders: "Bring on the puddles. Find more ice."

THE MASKS WE WEAR

When I was seven, I recall sitting at the dinner table on this sacred night, Halloween, and wondering how my father could be late. Didn't he know that the most exciting evening of the year was about to unfold? How could he walk through the door at the last moment having so little regard for the hours of anticipation and preparation that went into the magic of the annual ghost festival.

In a few minutes I would be transformed. Putting on my mask (that particular year it was Zorro's), my entire person would change. No longer a shy, bumbling boy, I would become the dark and agile knight of justice. I suppose today, it would be a power ranger, Ninja turtle or Disneyesque hunchback that would capture our children's imaginations. No matter the character, the metamorphosis is the same.

Masks make mountains out of mole hills, princes from toads and radiant sleeping beauties from shy wallflowers.

The reigning wisdom on Halloween masks is shifting. Where once the ponderous cover-your-whole-face variety were acceptable, now the politically correct toddler goes in for discreet and tiny facial coverings. Ideally a mask should be as transparent as possible and allow the child a clear line of vision. Smaller is better. Any heavy obstructions which might make the movement of the head difficult should be avoided. Stay away from any plastic or cloth masks which might fall over a child's eyes. Why not try face paint or heavy make-up? In the end, the best mask is no mask at all.

It works for kids and what good advice for adults.

Grown-ups don't wait for Halloween. Every morning we rise and put on another face. You've seen them and worn them, haven't you? There's the "cold, business-as-usual" mask. Who doesn't try on the "I-have-my-act-together" masquerade? At the very least, we all don the "tight-tie-and-well-pressed-skirt-that-spells-prosperity" disguise. We've used them all and they can be quite cumbersome, if not down right dangerous.

When we venture out into the wider world with our mask fixed tightly to our face, the chief impediments are not the raging traffic which we cannot see nor hidden obstacles waiting to trip us when our head is turned. Like Halloween fantasies of all kinds, the problem with masks is that we begin to believe them.

When I was a child I became Zorro or Superman. There was no distinction between the hero outside and boy inside. So too as an adult. The longer I wear the put-together pretence, the longer I believe it. The real danger of masks is not how they change our outward appearance, but the fact that they alter our inward perceptions. We actually invest our self-worth in a deception of our own creating. When I dress in that tight-as-a-drum suit, I actually believe I am important. The world would stop, if I didn't show up at the office. When you come to the shopping mall in that rock hard shell of gaiety, you really believe that you can live the Hollywood life. No blemishes or bruises please. And we all know the panic of wondering which made-up face we showed to which audience.

Call me crazy, but after a while I begin to trust my mask more than the real me inside. In fact, there are times when I can't even distinguish when the ruse begins and I end—smudged together into a blur. In the end I lose the essential "me" in the confusing round of my daily Mardi Gras life. And then who am I really—a succession of shallow spoofs?

Maybe modern Halloween masks should come with a disclaimer: "Warning: The Wearing of Masks can be Harmful to the Soul." "Danger: Masquerading can be addictive."

I'm not against fun. Don't paint me with that moralistic brush. Just a piece of Halloween advice. When the play has ended, take off the mask. No matter how dreamy we are with them on, or how dowdy or naked we feel with them off, we all look much better without deception. The real thing—-that's beautiful.

FOR JAMIE ...

Jamie, you were the kind of kid who lived on the edge. Over the boards and dash down the ice. Jump in the canoe and paddle like crazy. That was your style. It's no wonder your headstrong attitude sometimes landed you in the drink—literally. I suspect your suicide was in the same ballpark, over before it started.

It is only as we climb out of our teenage tempests that we realize death is for keeps. There won't be a morning after, no second chance. If we drive too close to the brink, the rescue mission may not arrive in time to drag us back. All that remains is a profound silence, a break in the chain of relationships.

Jamie, your death is a tragedy on so many levels. Initially, I feel as if life itself has failed you. In spite of all the promises this earth can offer from a loving Creator, some people believe they have no option but to leave it. Of course, there are instances when we have been so hurt by betrayal, gossip or abuse, that ending it all seems like the only solution. (The only decision worth contemplating, according to Jean-Paul Sartre.) But whether we succeed or fail, the attempt to take one's life is like a barometer of this world's attractiveness. The fact that many teenagers seek to leave behind embodied existence is a measure of our failure to impart the beauty and potential of living.

And, Jamie, I know you knew about the delights of life on this planet. That's what makes it all so damnable. You knew the strength of community through a church youth group that always befriended you, a girlfriend with whom you shared joint custody of a new puppy, and especially your family. You could feel, touch and taste the bounty that surrounded you.

But you were a loner. And that brings up the second tragedy. It's not as though your suicide was unpredictable. I hold in my mind a picture of a solitary child spending his summer holidays on the river by his home. Alone, except for the fish you regularly caught, you were a sitting duck for the stalking temptation of suicide. On trips to the movie theatre or sitting at our breakfast table, we knew how fragile your defences could be.

We were there at your baptism, your first day of kindergarten, the day you went on your first wilderness trip, but we couldn't be there to silence the schoolyard barbs nor protect you from the jabs that hurt so much. We helped you through some rocky times. I recall dragging you from the freezing waters of the river on a youth group kayak trip. So why couldn't we pull you out this last time? Upon further reflection, your suicide was also tragic because it was so pointless. Do we need a funeral to know how much you meant to our community? The young women who spoke in praise of your goofy ways and tender heart meant what they said. They will miss you and treasure what you gave to them. You were loved. Since the service, I've talked with people who knew you as a child. They mourn your passing deeply. The folks in the choir were left speechless. You meant a great deal to them, more than you realized. If only you had been able to remember and hang on to that goodwill when the storms of self-doubt hit.

Jamie, in a strange way, I want to declare that it's not your fault. You're not to blame. The past practice of casting shame upon those who attempt or commit suicide is misplaced. Religious imperatives are unhelpful. There is no sin here, just tears and deep regret.

So what next? Is there any meaning I can draw from this multi-layered tragedy? I am cautious about finding a moral to end this dark story. If anything, your dying underlined the essence of your living. The zest and rush with which you attacked each sunrise are watchwords for those of us who remain at the close of the day. You showed us that there's no time like the present to do the things we want, say what we mean, and express our deepest feelings for those we love. We need to make the most of our daylight hours and feel your energy in our striving.

You knew that lesson, lived by that rule, and we'll honour you by keeping it.

Love, Chris

I BUILD BOATS FOR PEOPLE TO USE

It looks like a piece of furniture, polished smooth to a hair's breadth, bird's-eye maple struts, ash decks—this is really a canoe! So fine is the craftsmanship that it wouldn't be out of place in the most elegant of salons.

Visitors to the northern New Brunswick shop where

these beauties are born might pause. Wood chips, paddle shavings, hand drills, bolts of canvas and cedar planks lie about in an unholy jumble. How can such precision emerge from this clutter? My favourite, an 18-foot Chickadee, "dances on the water," according to Bill, its maker. And he manages to make a perfect creation every time. Nothing is missing. No smudge in the paint is too small to buff out. Mosquito nicks on the gunnels are burnished away. At the end of three weeks of sweat mixed with inspiration, out comes a floating piece of art.

Remarkably modest, Bill runs his hands over his wares and admits, "It ain't perfect yet, but each one is better than the last." To an amateur's eye, I can't see much room for improvement.

"It looks good enough to hang on the wall," is my contribution to a steady flow of compliments, which Bill enjoys. But this brings a serious wrinkle in his usually light brow. "No, that would be wrong. I didn't make these boats for people to put them in a museum. I want to have kids walking up and down in them as they go down the river. Why would you build canoes if they weren't ever going to see water?"

Indeed, any master crafter, one intimately acquainted with creating, longs to see the fruit of their labour enjoyed and shared with others.

According to scripture, God feels the same way.

It is, therefore, surprising when believers consign some of the best heavenly oeuvre d'arts to celestial confinement.

Take sex as a primary example of one of God's most ingenious and pleasing creations. It has been assumed by generations of religious ascetics that the best sacrifice we can make for our faith is to forego the "bodily pleasures." Making the argument that bodily matters are dirty, base and distracting, human sexuality has been cloaked in a mantle of foreboding. Preachers and priests drilled home the dictum that the "lusts of the flesh" are among the vilest of mortal sins.

But deep emotions cannot be banished so simply. In reality, the Christian ban on sexuality has simply driven our desires underground. Consequently, the charms over human embodiment were corrupted. Rather than being shared and explored in an atmosphere of honesty and delight, sex was whispered in unholy ways, twisted and used to perversion.

If we look for an explanation of the recent disclosures over the sexual impropriety of religious leaders, a good deal of blame rests with a theological tradition which could not rejoice openly in this fundamental gift of God, but felt constrained to suppress it.

In less dramatic fashion, the religious tendency to relegate sex to a don't-touch-and-don't-taste status has meant that many disciples of Christ still titter in guilt and insecurity when sexual feelings are expressed. Weighed down by this anchor of sexual insecurity, we have made many mistakes.

My friend Bill would never want his canoes to be mishandled or subjected to dangerous or frivolous exercises. The same is true of sex. It is not a lightweight issue.

Nevertheless, at the heart of human pornography, sexual abuse and even minor misunderstandings lies a great religious mistake. God does not hate sex. It is not too vulgar for our worshipping communities. On the contrary, sex is a gift to be enjoyed, a very beautiful craft to be tested and used.

WHEN THE WIND BLOWS WHO STANDS FIRM?

It began as an ordinary outdoor wedding. The bride was from a small rural village and wished to grace her special day with the memories of that pastoral peace. Given the progressive maturity of the small community, weddings were rare and so everyone turned out to help, each hoping to have greater part in the ceremony than their neighbour. Every detail was checked and double-checked. Cakes were baked, sandwiches made. This was to be a party to end all parties.

There was no way to guarantee the weather so the bride's family wisely, as it turned out, ordered a large caravan tent to protect the guests in the unlikely event of rain.

Come the day and everyone gathered. Storm clouds were looming on the horizon, but it was generally agreed they wouldn't dare spoil such a momentous occasion.

Everything was ironed, tied or iced waiting for the 2:00 p.m. arrival of the minister and the people "from away."

In the morning there was some uncertainty, call it last minute jitters, on the part of the groom who, seeing the looming weather, had the ceremony switched to a chapel at the crossroads. But by 12:30 the sun was still peeking out from behind the clouds and so the family changed his mind. "After all, if it gets sprinkly," the bride's father argued, "they could all just move under the tent."

The appointed hour arrived along with some ominous thunder clouds, but it looked like God was hovering near for there was not a drop of rain in the air. Looking over her shoulder at this ominous warning, I think the minister went through the service with as much haste as decorum would allow. They kissed each other, pronounced themselves joined for love and life and were just beginning to sign the register when the first drops fell. No problem. The beauty of the out-of-doors had been enjoyed by all and then the party smoothly moved into the tent to finish the technical details and get down to some serious partying.

The tent was decked out in flowers, ribbons, balloons and cake. The guests found their places at white linen table settings. The bride flowed into the tent in a gown of silk and happiness, the groom was gleeful and the minister dragging the registry books for a final signature from both.

Then it hit. Hail storms don't usually give much warning and this one was typical. Almost like a hammer, the rain and small pellets hit the roof. As if by prearranged signal, everyone looked up. Would the tent hold? After a second or two of doubt, it was clear that the canvas was strong enough and there was a collective sigh.

Then the wind picked up. It was pretty strong and at first the guy wires seemed to be holding things tight. It beat against the plastic awnings that served as windows and knawed at the ground floor edges.

Then in one disastrous puff, the tempest curled under one, and then two, and then all sides of the canvas and whirled up to the roof top. It didn't stop at the ceiling but kept pushing until the tent poles came undone from their moorings, the guy wires went slack and the shelter col-lapsed. Cake, candles, bride, minster, registry, guests all were draped in wet canvas and from the outside it looked like a misshapen, multi-headed ghost.

It was the worst possible scenario. The bride was in tears, the groom got angry, but the guests got busy. While the wedding party was being dusted off in the living room of the house, comforted with "now don't" and "we'll see," another cake was produced (country folk are nothing if not prepared). As if by magic, the balloons and flowers were rescued from under the under mess on the lawn. Tablecloths were whisked away to be ironed flat, chairs and tables sprouted in the local community hall. Everyone pitched in. A messenger was sent to the local general store. "Tell Paul to send down all the streamers he's got." Paul did. In fact, he brought them himself even though he was not acquainted with the couple. Under his arm were some fireworks for the later evening, a couple of bags of candy for children and a bottle of gin for the bride's father. Paul didn't know him, but was certain he would need it.

By the time the tears were dried in the bride's house, the local hall was a palace of light and colour. The food, which inexplicably had not been taken into the ill-fated tent, reappeared at neatly set place settings. It was as if nothing was amiss.

You might say that the miracle of the day was that the wedding could be salvaged so well and you might be right. But from my perspective, the real presence of the divine in that day was the spirit of community that went to work on behalf of a disappointed young couple. It's not five-inch headline material, but in its own way it is what makes the world worth saving. God bless 'em.

5 THE QUESTIONS YOU'VE ALWAYS WANTED TO ASK

DOES GOD EXIST? PROOF #1

Is God dead? Until very recently, our cynical,tough-minded society regarded this as a rhetorical question. Of course God is dead. Not only has "He" been proven to be little more than a misguided psychological projection of human insecurity, God is no longer needed as a working hypothesis when examining the cosmos. Building on the discoveries of the enlightenment, this century's value-free science has uncovered the basic dynamics of nature, and an all-powerful deity is superfluous.

The modern consumer culture—child of the technological revolution—has also made God unnecessary. Our general well-being is assured through advances in travel, medicine and urban living. Progress is written right into our history so that every new product is also "improved." Give us just a few more decades, and we will solve all our social problems. It's inevitable.

Is it any surprise that our best and brightest adhered to something like a benign disregard of religious principles while constructing this brave new world that would meet all our needs? Who needs silly, outdated superstitions? Without the assistance of an Almighty Creator, we can build a culture of plenty in which the deserving will always find work, honesty will never go unrewarded, children will be cherished and nurtured with compassion, and our elders will enjoy security and peace.

That was the great dream. But today's reality is sadly lacking in the "All Things Bright and Beautiful" picture painted by the architects of our modern world. Despair rather than contentment has become everyone's mother tongue. Sociological studies indicate that rates of depression are doubling in some industrial countries every 10 years. Suicide is currently the third most common cause of death among young adults in North America. It is estimated that out of ten women attending university, two are anorexic and six are bulimic. We are, indeed, a desperate people! At the close of a millennium, we now see that the great godless vision of bounty and light is bankrupt.

It is this epidemic of despair that is motivating a resurgence of spiritual interest. God is on the rebound. There are many folk, from plumbers to pediatricians, turning to get a second opinion on religion. Perhaps there is more to living than buying and selling. Maybe we were a bit hasty when we pronounced God dead on arrival. Is it possible that "She," "He," or "It" is still in business?

There are several traditional arguments for the existence of God, and I have been interested to see the resurgence of scientific research supporting a few of these theories. Take the teleological proof for the existence of God as an example. Basically, medieval scholars argued that the created order gives evidence of a hidden purpose. There is a pattern to the cycle of the seasons and the rhythm of life and death. The universe is not a pinball machine where random chance is the dominant and directing force. On the contrary. There's a hidden hand directing the planets in their courses. Ergo—God exists.

Recently, a similar theme has emerged among hard-nosed physicists and mathematicians who are pushing the edges of our understanding of time and creation. They call it the Anthropic Cosmological Principle and suggest that from all the countless possible courses of its evolution, the universe took the only one that enabled life to emerge. Why is that? Is it not strange or even miraculous that a whirling dust cloud of atoms moved in such a fashion as to make life happen? For such scientists as Stephen Hawking, Rupert Sheldrake or James Lovelock, the theological implications are impossible to ignore. Something was or is guiding the stars and moon. Whether accepting the old theory or the new one, the basic concept is the same. Life is not simply a chance encounter. There is a purposeful direction guiding the entire universe, if not our specific lives.

I don't offer this resurgence in God-talk as a quick-fix remedy for the deep discontent that grips our culture. Despair is not that easily cured, but our generation may well be appreciating for the first time since the industrial age that we are limited as a species. Lasting strength and meaning must come from beyond our grasp. We are discovering that this world is not our playground, to be used and abused for our amusement, and that spiritual depth is as essential as material wealth.

Hallelujah!

As yet I don't know how to pray to an Anthropic Cosmological Principle, but it begins to give me a pinch of assurance to know that theologians and scientists are both confessing that we are not castaways on a careening, out-of-control planet. It's not a blinding light—not yet. But I can feel an inkling of hope.

GUILT:
HANDLE WITH CARE

Guilt is like spiritual dynamite, a psycho-emotional explosive just waiting to go off. What you do with it can be a matter of life and death.

You feel guilty because you don't spend enough time with your family and that sense of remorse blows up all over some unsuspecting colleague at work. You know you should have spoken a word of forgiveness to the person on the other end of the phone, and your guilt implodes—scattering doubt and regret all over your self image.

Guilt, while it may not be as pervasive as was once the case, is still one of the most potent and most common diseases to afflict the human heart. We all know how it feels. Like a dead weight around the neck or a rumbling stone in the stomach. Whether it's caused by broken relationships, unfinished work, or unthinking acts, the "should" of guilt troubles everyone. In many cases our guilt drives us to depression and self-doubt, and in some extreme circumstances it has pushed people into suicide. No small matter!

In many ways, religion is an organized response to guilt. We look to an outside source, a great Creator, as a second opinion. In communion with the source of all life, we find respite from our nagging sense of culpability. At their best, the world's major faith traditions have eased the burden, devising ways for people to seek and receive forgiveness, relief from the ache of having fallen short of what we intended to be.

At their worst, religious traditions have used guilt as a hook, snaring people in their soft spots, never giving release until the devout gave all they had to preserve the religious machinery. What a dreadful history we religious folks have to live down—the mountains of guilt we have constructed: "Thou shalt's" and "Thou shalt not's."

Wholesome faith isn't interested in guilt since guilt creates nothing. Like an explosive, it can do only one thing—blow up, leave a gaping hole in your heart. So when someone pushes your guilt button, they get an immediate reaction—lots of smoke and a good deal of fire but that's it. After the flash there's nothing left.

Would you take your car to someone who only had dynamite as a tool? The human soul is infinitely more intricate than an automobile and deserves greater care. Contrary to popular belief, making people feel guilt doesn't help them to change their behaviour. Ironically, it binds us all the more firmly to that which we detest in ourselves. Some say that guilt serves exactly this purpose. To use a popular example, we know we shouldn't have too much cheesecake, but we crave it regularly. Feeling guilty is the price we pay for not changing our eating habits.

Faith, when it is life-giving, draws people away from guilt to responsibility. They grow very closely together.

Guilt hides, pretends, and stands still. Responsibility names, accepts and moves on. The chief question is: Do you want to get free of guilt? That's not a simple question. But if you do, then explain your shortcomings to the person you have offended, accept your part (and only your part) in the brokenness and accept that you must move on. It is easy to write about and so much more difficult to live out.

In the final analysis, I am able to live out my responsibility only because I sense within creation a cycle of forgiveness. Winter, spring, day, night beat out a rhythm of forgiveness that signals a new beginning for everyone.

The next time you see guilt lying about in your own soul, in your church, home or place of work, remember it's an explosive. Take this advice, handle it with care and avoid it if at all possible. Responsibility is much more stable and life-giving.

STAMP OUT "WORM" THEOLOGY

Have you ever noticed how the good we intend becomes bad, how our best intentions lead to misery? Here's an example.

There once was an isolated community on Martha's Vineyard, an island off the coast of Massachusetts, in which a genetic anomaly had caused one in every ten people to be born deaf. Apparently, it arrived with the first settlers in the 1600s and intermarriage kept the occurrence of deafness at a constant level for many years.

Before this remarkable situation was dissipated through contact with the wider world, there was a study done which indicated that, miracle of miracles, the hearing community and non-hearing community were virtually indistinguishable. The island people had developed their own unique sign language and, consequently, equal numbers of hearing and non-hearing folk graduated from high school, married and had children. Likewise, the two groups enjoyed similar standards of living and participated without distinction in all varieties of work. Indeed, it was quite remarkable!

When compared with the rest of the state, which was known at the time for its advanced services to the deaf, the island community's achievement was astounding. In the mainland population, only 50 per cent of non-hearing individuals graduated from high school as compared with 75 per cent of the wider populace. The marriage rate of non-hearing people outside Martha's Vineyard was no better than half that of the general public, and only 40 per cent of non-hearing families had children. This discouraging inequality was echoed throughout all the social indicators.

How can it be that on an island with no services, non-hearing and hearing people were equal, while in the society just 30 miles away with an army of sophisticated services at its disposal, deaf folk lived a much poorer, more marginalized existence than the hearing community? Is it possible that the services we offer, rather than solving the problem, produce the opposite effect? Does our help, benevolent as it may be, keep people where they are, stuck in their misery?

Using this case of the hearing and non-hearing communities, some social activists suggest that we focus too much on deficiency, in this case deafness, and not enough on healing. We concentrate on what's wrong rather than on what's right; too much effort on what is, rather than what could be.

Now comes the time for confession. While I am not a judge of social services for the non-hearing community. I have all too often used my religion in exactly that "deficiency-driven" pattern—as a tool to examine what's wrong with the world rather than as a means to celebrate what's right.

For centuries, Christians particularly have looked upon human beings as "worms five feet high," and under the guise of this "truth," have pulverized many weak and trembling souls. We argued that people couldn't do anything right and had no hope of salvation, apart from God's action. This "worm" theology, well intentioned as it might once have been, has caused untold damage on all believers, but particularly on those who lack power— women, the poor, the immigrant. Their political and social oppression was justified by the religion which only saw their sickness and imputed wickedness, and never spoke of their healing and intrinsic worthiness.

Ever so slowly, this punishing religion is changing. Largely through the efforts of marginalized believers themselves—women, people of colour, the poor—there is a new wind blowing. Prayers now begin with rejoicing for what is good and life-giving. Hearts and minds bend toward the celebration of what is to be cherished both in human life and in creation. We religious types have been deaf for too long!

IN PRAISE OF WISDOM Clyde is proud of his 81 years. He still walks half a mile each evening, drives his own truck, chops most of his own firewood, and is a very learned fellow. He knows why the salmon are unable to spawn in the river outside his New Brunswick dooryard. He can tell you how to whittle wooden fans from a single piece of cedar and can recite bible stories from memory. What he knows cannot be found in books but must be learned from experience. Clyde is a guide, a farmer, a sawyer, a lumberman and a soldier, all wrapped into one. But these days it is his considerable skill as a storyteller that attracts most visitors. His memory can reach back into the mists of time and pull out the most bizarre characters— famous fishermen, old buddies from the lumber camps. Quite a host of witnesses!

To enjoy more of Clyde's tales, I dropped by for a visit with no special purpose; it was just a friendly call. We had just finished discussing those run-of-the-mill topics like the weather and everyone's health when he mentioned his book. "Did I want to see it?" In a twinkling, he produced a much-prized volume of his finest poems—they'd been submitted to the poetry contest of the 1992 Literacy Competition of the Writers' Federation of New Brunswick. Who would have thought that under the leathered exterior of a hard working woodsman there lived a poet?

The first selection entitled "Religion" caught my eye. When I looked up to offer a word of praise, I caught the glint in Clyde's eye. This was no casual circumstance. He was waiting for my reaction.

Now in most instances when people hand "the minister" a creative piece, it's usually some well-meaning, often sentimental rendition of a pious melody from the last century. Not so with Clyde. In lyrical honesty, he begins to survey the major themes in the bible's creation narrative —what it means to him, how it relates to the world of mice and men that he has known. But rather than finding a carefully constructed harmonious ending, he concludes with a question:

Now if Cain and Eve and Adam
Were all that's left of life,
Where in hell did Cain go
To find himself a wife?

Clearly, Clyde sees more than meets the eye. With an integrity which has marked his life's work, he has uncovered a hole in the scripture's neatly woven fabric. Where did Cain find a partner if Adam and Eve were the first human beings on earth? The question can be answered by some biblical gymnastics, no doubt. However, I have never pondered it too deeply. Like Clyde, I sense that Cain's marital dilemma doesn't need a response. It's just one loose end that is left hanging after a very interesting tale is told.

Reading Clyde's final verse over again, I wonder if he's being a bit ironic—using that one scriptural "error" to point out that we must be careful when reading Holy writ. One mustn't take these tales too literally, for they won't hold up to close scrutiny. By extension, you could argue that one mustn't take the whole religious exercise too seriously.

I sit for a moment perched on a stool in Clyde's porch and marvel at his wisdom. Without theological training, he has discovered a fundamental truth of the bible. Its stories are meant to be lights to brighten our lives, to cast out shadows and reveal goodness, but they are not meant as literal prescriptions for daily living. Clyde knows all this because he himself is a storyteller. The fish are always "this" big (hands held wide apart) and the old days are always "good" (head nodding wisely).

In an instant-replay culture, this appreciation of story has been lost. People who are raised on cold, hard facts are unable to hear the wisdom of his verse. They look at a book like the bible and read it word for word like a history text. How sad!

Thank goodness, thank God for the poets of this world who keep wisdom alive.

THE BIG BUT

When I was very young, life was free of conditions. There were no "buts" clouding the horizon. It was only later as I became an adolescent that I learned the actual phrase, "There's no such thing as a free lunch." As qualifiers were imposed on my actions and my ambitions, I felt the "but" spirit muddying the clear running water of my daily routine. "You can go out to play, but you must clean up your room first." "You may have a party, but you must end it all by midnight." "You can have as much ice cream as you like, but you must leave enough for everyone."

"Buts" can be helpful, indeed essential, for they corral our extravagant passions and tie down wild ideas which otherwise might be damaging. A well placed "but" can be a sobering second thought or a check on selfish indulgence, while an ethical "but" can inspire an indulgent heart to feel the legitimate claims of a wider community.

"Buts" are an important tool in the mechanics of ethical and spiritual thinking, but ... but, there are times and places where the "but" gets in the way or misdirects the flow of believing. I'm thinking of one specific "but" used by institutionalized religion which has had disastrous results—the "but" of conditional acceptance. Here's a living example.

Alice arrived at my office door near tears. From past encounters, I knew she carried around a boat-load of "buts." Her story came back to me as she took a seat—the "buts" of a family life where she was the central care giver.

She stayed single and watched her youth disappear as she cared first for her ailing parents and then her bachelor brothers. The world of romance and excitement called, "but" she made the beds, washed the floors and prepared all the meals without fail. She yearned to be free, "but" she played her role as the dutiful servant of others. Work wasn't much better, for the "buts" followed her. There were many demands in her low paying job. She wanted to go out in the evening, maybe watch a movie, "but" she stayed late and did the extra work as it came along. Higher education beckoned, "but" she couldn't quit and let her boss down.

Alice followed a similar pattern in the church. She attended regularly, contributed her tithe to God's work and supplied cookies for every bake sale and spring tea. She kept faith and did what she should do. That's what the Almighty expected in return for eternal blessings. What a ponderous chain of obligations hung around her neck, forged as the necessary conditions of being loved and accepted by others and by God.

Now in my office, I could see it breaking down. While sitting with outward patience, I could tell that Alice's tolerance for the "buts" of her life was wearing thin. There was a slight twitch at the edges of her smile betraying the calm exterior. "I've come to see you about that awful sermon." (Alice was always direct!) "I haven't stopped thinking about it." You say God's love is unconditional, but I've grown up knowing what I should do and what God requires of me. To get love you have to be good. Isn't that what God wants?" In her razor sharp manner, she had articulated the "but of conditional acceptance." Your family will love willingly, but you must prove your devotion first. Your employers will accept you, but you must "go the second mile" to retain that acceptance. God loves you, but expects some pretty strict measures to be followed, or else! Her life had been a litany of "buts."

Alice, you've been religiously abused! There is no "but" to God's love. It is. It gives without counting the cost. It receives without prerequisite. It is as extravagant as it is irrational. God loves—full stop, period, no conditions. Consequently, love from our Creator can never be bought—not by gifts, nor right actions, nor politically correct thinking. Love is and is without price. When we place a "but" after it, we distort it into obligation.

DOES GOD REALLY EXIST? PROOF #2

It's the middle of the night. Long shadows are falling across my daytime assurances. Eyes wide open, I stare at the ceiling and face the fact that life hangs by a thread. A speeding car or latent cancer can change everything in a twinkling of an eye. Lightning or fire could strike this house, and I could go to sleep this evening and never wake up.

When these nocturnal nightmares hit, who doesn't

strive to see beyond the darkness into the eternal? Is human existence just one long joke, or is there someone, something guiding it all? Does God really exist, or are we imagining things? Maybe God is dead and all our prayers are worthless babbling.

Here's a two-part story which responds to this very natural anxiety over proof about God's existence.

There once was an expert mountain climber who ventured onto an isolated and dangerous stretch of the Alps. Being confident in his skill and the day having dawned without a cloud in the sky, he was undisturbed by the serious difficulties that lay ahead. Indeed, he fared quite well throughout the morning and arrived at his destination with very little trouble. As is often the case, going up was easy, but coming down was another story. The mountain turned a bitter and unrelenting face toward this solitary figure clinging to the rocks. A northern storm slowly crept over the mountain range, whipping sharp-edged rain into his face. Gripping the handholds with frozen fingers, he began to lose heart. His nerves snapped—toeholds gave way, and he began to fall. If it hadn't been for a rope he had wedged into a crevice minutes before, he would have fallen to his death. He was hanging, quite literally, "at the end of his rope" watching the verdant green valley below sway back and forth between his dangling feet.

In desperation he cried out into the abyss, "Help ... help ... is anyone out there?" ... Silence ... "Help ... please. I'm desperate and alone ... is anyone out there?"

Hold this picture in your mind. It's not all that

remarkable nor surprising that an individual beyond hope would reach out to the Almighty for protection. "Where are you God?" It's an instinctive reflex of most human beings.

This reflex, to reach beyond ourselves, is known in theological circles as the ontological proof for the existence of God. Almost a thousand years ago, a religious thinker argued that we know there is a God precisely because, like the mountain climber, the very fact that human beings have the instinctive idea of God built right into their being is evidence of God's existence. (The Greek word for "being" is ontos, hence, the idea of an "ontological" proof.) The actual formula of this "proof" is convoluted, but its meaning is simple. The notion of a higher power crops up as a universal principle in every culture, leaving footprints in all human hearts. This is the best evidence for our Creator's existence.

Such thinking is not confined to the ancient mystics. Recent medical studies of near-death experiences indicate that there is a striking similarity in the perceptions of those who have returned to life after being declared dead. Most recount a feeling of deep contentment and feather-light joy. There is often a beckoning light and a sense of being called away from the embodied world. Such similarities suggest a design, a pattern or purpose—one controlled or created by a greater Power.

Now comes the second part of our story. It illustrates the danger of this proof for the existence of God.

The mountain climber is hanging from a strand of

nylon. He has called out for God, "Is there anyone out there? Please help me."

Miraculously, through the howling winds comes a reassuring and resonant response. "Yes my son, I am here; you are not alone. Don't be afraid, for I will protect you. Let go of the rope."

The mountain climber paused and then shouted,"Is there anyone else out there?" What we do with this primordial reflex is often bizarre, if not dangerous. We can, like the mountain climber, turn our instinctive concept of God into a great Santa Claus in the sky—someone who gives us what we want when we want it. Such a childlike fabrication relieves us of any responsibility for our actions, and if we are not careful, we can twist this deity into a monster to afflict our enemies.

The Buddhists have a saying which acts as a check on our God reflex. They agree that deep insight is a central component of human life, and realize that God is more than our personal perceptions. Consequently, they argue that if you see Buddha coming down the road, kill him, for that is not the real Buddha. Don't be fooled by your images of God. Wise counsel, especially for mountain climbers.

WHEN LIFE ENDS

"So, how are you? How was your summer?"

It was a chance encounter beginning with that innocent greeting. I wasn't intending to go any further than the day-by-day exchange of pleasantries, but a cloud settles over her face. This is obviously difficult.

"Actually," she says, "It wasn't good at all, since my father died in late July."

Now, I've done it! Feeling a knot forming in my stomach, I wonder what to say next. Is there any word which doesn't sound trite or too impersonal to those who have experienced the death of a loved one? Who isn't apprehensive when confronted by those who mourn? Are there any guides for those who face the bereaved—first aid rules to follow when life ends and grieving begins?

It isn't an exhaustive list, but here are a few hints about the do's and don'ts of encountering those who stand at the grave side.

DO name the pain. It's not rocket science, just common sense.

A comment on the difficulty of death can be exactly to the point. Many people believe they can deal best with death by pretending it away. That's a bad idea, since buried grief festers, eventually causing irreparable damage. It's much healthier to say it. Death hurts. It's the end of a unique conversation, and no matter how much we may be expecting life to end, death interrupts the dialogue. Anger, love, guilt, pleasure, fear, regret—whatever we're feeling, death leaves it dangling. We cannot face and sort out these emotions until we name them.

DO ask how it happened. Rather than being idle curiosity, a question about the circumstances of death is a way to share the pain. Suffering is like a heavy load carried by the grieving, a sack of "shoulds," "if-onlys" and "could-have-beens." When we share in the details of the final days, we quite literally shoulder some of their burden. As the grieving retell their story, they transfer some of the pain to their audience. One of the great blessings of community is its capacity to absorb suffering.

DO enquire about past history. If you have time and opportunity, you can progress beyond the immediate circumstances of death to talk about the particulars of life. "How did you first meet?" "What were your special days?" Again, this is not morbid or prying but a way of evaluating the life that was. Weighing the high points, cherishing the funny stories, and recalling the shining hours are very needful steps on the road to the celebration and thanksgiving for the miracles of living.

DON'T whistle in the dark. Sometimes we suggest that the lost person is "sleeping" or "passed away," and we think we are being polite and respectful to the grieving. In fact, we're hiding from our own anxiety and fear. Similarly, it is unfair to make light of an anticipated death. Long struggles with cancer or creeping old age doesn't mean that the final break will be any less sharp or hurtful.

DON'T try to play God and find a reason for any specific death. It is hard to resist. We would all like to assure the bereaved person with an answer to the "why" question. Surely, there is some way to make this death make sense. "Heaven needs her." "He's out of his suffering now." "God wanted her more than us." All too often, these are empty gestures which are more prone to raise false hopes than lasting assurance. It's better not to offer facile solutions to life's misfortunes.

DON'T back away. You may have trouble saying anything and you might be too shy to follow any of the above suggestions. That's okay. Just hold your ground. Sometimes the best and only thing we can do is to wait with people in their hardship. It is said that a picture is better than a thousand words. Well, a sympathetic presence is worth a million well rehearsed phrases.

All these "dos" and "don'ts" are useless without one essential ingredient—compassion. All the technique in world is useless without it. Without compassion, all our daily greetings are empty. With it, they are the avenues to healing and wholeness.

GOD'S SILENCE OVER HUMAN SUFFERING

There is some suffering which is beyond belief, and it's the best argument for the non-existence of God.

Sharon had called the pastor in tears. It was hard to distinguish the jumble of words as waves of deep sobs washed over her. As she gasped for air and meaning, it was clear she needed help. Would he come over right away?

Arriving at what was a typical suburban home, the minister discovered a litany of horrors. There was blood on the driveway, the car in a skid on the lawn, and a crowd of neighbours blocking the front door of the house. Ambulance lights were flickering red and white across their shocked faces. Inside, orange suits worked on the small, still form of a two-year-old boy.

Sharon and her partner had had yet another dispute. Their marriage had been falling apart, and its collapse was evident even when they had come to the church recently to have the child baptized.

Now this!

The tension had been building for weeks until it exploded. In a blind rage, she had stormed from the family home, leaving her husband inside with the broken tea cups and anger. Getting into the family car, she had backed out of the garage unseeing and had run over her two-year-old son.

The paramedics were doing all they could, but it took only a glance to realize the child would never recover. The husband was transfixed, staring into the abyss. Sharon was shedding tears of remorse and self-hatred that would take her more than a lifetime to overcome. It was no one's fault and everyone's fault.

At moments like this, the question on all minds, particularly of those who are religious is: "Is there a God?" When evil seems to triumph so completely, it is much easier to believe in the devil. Was the Creator of the Universe so callous as to allow a young life to be so easily extinguished? Was the Lover of Life temporarily absent from earthly affairs, leaving the front yard unattended, so to speak?

When great calamity strikes, where is God?

There should be a sign hung on that question: "DANGER! ENTER AT YOUR OWN RISK!"

Of course, there are religious people who will say that adversity is God's megaphone, a way to awaken our slumbering senses and make us alive to the fleeting nature of life. Maybe disaster of this magnitude is also a lesson to teach us faithfulness or direct our efforts toward love rather than hate. You could even argue that the death of the guileless is a way for God to reclaim God's own. But finding any reasonable answer to the dilemma of innocent suffering is an invitation to either trivialize the depth of our anguish or to turn God into a tyrant.

Surely, our initial response to suffering must and should be protracted silence. I am not counselling that we ignore our pain nor try to escape it through inaction. On the contrary, as we walk through the valley of the shadow, we say nothing because we want to hallow God's silence. If God is as compassionate and loving as we claim, then surely God is grieving just as we are over a young life snuffed out in its infancy. Let us give time for the Almighty to weep.

Just as we reach out to one another in our anguish, can we not reach out to a God in pain? When we hold each other, do we not hold God as well? As naive and paradoxical as that may seem, perhaps being in community is the only response to suffering. Perhaps creating a circle of solidarity and love with each other and with God is the final antidote to our broken hearts and the only way heaven can come to earth.

WHAT IF I NEVER GO TO CHURCH?

"Is Dad going to hell?" That's what Mary wondered in her quiet moments after the funeral. If any of the children asked, she would tell them that he was a faithful man, devout and kind, but he never went to church and had no time for religion. Nevertheless he wasn't going to hell.

That seemed to satisfy their childlike concerns, but Mary was still confused and angry. Now that Ivan, her father, was dead there was no chance for a reversal of his behaviour. In contrast to her dad, she had accepted the religious rules. Believe in God and you will be blessed … Go to church and God will protect you … Be humble and you will receive your reward in heaven." Only with maturing years did she discover that it doesn't work like that. Ivan had not been a believer and had never contributed to a religious organization that she could remember, but it was impossible to see how he would be denied God's forgiveness and grace.

Mary's dad had been an honest, well-respected man.

An immigrant to this country he had made his way with pride and respect. Did these attributes count for nothing? Just because he didn't bow his knee before the Lord is no reason to think that he was rejected by God. You see, Ivan was unwilling to stomach the courses of humilation pie served up at church services. "You're a wretch, a sinner, unacceptable before the eyes of God." It didn't make sense. He could see that human beings were good and evil, some better than others, some worse, but generally speaking we're all trying to muddle through honestly using what gifts we have been given. Did our fallibility really irritate the Maker so much that each Sunday morning we should clothe ourselves in sackcloth and heap ashes upon our head? Does God really expect us to grovel for forgiveness?

No, Ivan had a more realistic appraisal of human living—one that took people at their word, trusted in their basic goodness, and was not surprised when things went wrong, just as he was not surprised when things went right. It disturbed him to see the false humility among religious folk and watch their posturing when a "man of the cloth" passed by. As far as Mary's father was concerned, religion got in the way all too often.

What was true for Ivan is still too true for many believers today. There is an unreality to organized religion which centres on a basic contradiction in its message. On the one hand, Christianity, to name only one religion, begins with a sour note when it refers to human beings. Before we're born, we're sinful. To belong to God's family, we must accept that we're fallen, misshapen or generally less than what God would want. Imagine if, as a child, you woke up each morning to be told that you're a disappointment. Those children who have suffered such abuse are the first to explain how damaging it can be. You lose self-confidence, household chores become a burden, and you're looking for a way to leave your parents or to act out your frustrations. If you choose to stay, life unravels into an endless quest for parental approval that never comes. What a way to die (or to live)!

On the other hand, Christians are also encouraged to present ourselves for worship in our best attire, putting on our Sunday sunrise personalities, portraying a life that has the best of intentions and motivations. Who doesn't feel the urge to be "good" in the presence of the Almighty? Anyone can tell you how hard it is to keep up the appearances of "goodness" when things are not good. We arrive at our place of worship all in a hurry, the children complaining that they don't want to go and the weights of family life still clinging to our shoulders. What a painful show!

So it is that believers such as Ivan feel pulled both ways at the same time, and they leave religion behind as a failed experiment. They ask in all faithfulness, what happened to the loving creator God who accepts us as we are—blemishes and all, who expects us simply to be as fully human as we can be—no religious super heroes, just decent folk? Imagine a religion that takes you warts and all and says "Well done thou good and faithful servant." Is that too much to ask? Ivan didn't think so!

THE TEN-STEP PROGRAM TO PRAYING

Ever wonder why we pray? As a child, maybe you knelt by your bed, closed your hands over your eyes and listened to a parental admonition to say your evening prayers. Did you peek out between your fingers, gazing into the shadows to find God? Did you strain your ears to catch a response to your pleas? What is prayer all about, and how do you do it right? Let me offer these "ten commandments" about praying that direct my prayer life and which you might find helpful.

First, Thou shalt use prayer to take a break.

Prayer is a strategic retreat from daily living. When we close our eyes or kneel on the carpet, we are shutting out the strains and stresses of the world. Call it a rest stop on the day's highway. Everyone's soul needs to find repose and a place to take a break from the noise and pressure of traffic, so to speak.

Second, Thou shalt think thy way into God's presence.

Prayer doesn't stand still. It begins when we try to think or feel our way toward God. There are no special "magical" words, no prescribed approach signals. Just begin to open your heart and mind to the Creator.

Resisting the temptation to clutter up the silence with verbiage is the best start.

Third, Thou shalt imagine thyself into a position where God can get at thee.

Prayer is about being fully present to God. Presbyterian Christians used to stand up when they prayed. Jews still do. In a symbolic way they are saying, "Okay, God, take your best shot. I can handle your judgments, and I'm not afraid to hear what you think of me." One dimension of prayer is critical in nature—being open to hear God's evaluation of us.

Fourth, Thou shalt be open to God praying in thee.

Prayer is not a one-way street, something only initiated by human beings. In the flutter of autumn leaves, in the grace-filled words of a friend, or in the crash of money markets, God may be praying into our world. Can we be so presumptuous to believe that God only waits for us to call?

Fifth, Thou shalt pray in communion.

Too often, prayer is a spectator sport where the "pros" do all the work. But it's meant to be participatory and a way to touch others, to re-connect with creation. In this sense, praying is a form of communing with the God that is embodied in the world around us. Who hasn't felt prayerful when walking through a spring forest or watching the sun rise on mountain slopes?

Sixth, Thou shalt not turn prayer into thy shopping list.

God is not Santa Claus and doesn't need to be supplied with a wish list of all your wants or needs. Such bargain basement approaches to prayer are self-serving and often hopeless attempts to bend God to our own ends. If God is really God, then God knows what you want before you speak.

Seventh, Thou shalt not use prayer to escape.

Don't hide in heaven. Prayer may be a tactical retreat from the world, but it is never an escape from life's problems. Indeed, it may be the very time and space in which we can comfortably and authentically assess the challenges of our lives. When we use prayer to run from earthly existence, we may miss the call of our Creator who speaks in the world around us.

Eighth, Thou shalt not turn praying into posturing.

God hates pretence—the empty show of piety. So don't turn your prayer into a show for others, a flourish of hands or the exaggerated humble pie posture designed to impress others with how devout you are. Hide in a closet if you feel tempted to this dramatic extravagance, since praying is fundamentally about honesty.

Ninth, Thou shalt not use prayer as a weapon.

Have you ever been prayed into a corner? Religious leaders of all stripes are guilty of this sin from time to time. They may not like what you've said, or they think their point was not clearly made in the sermon so they turn the "closing" prayer into another tool. Prayer is an inviting hand, not a threatening fist.

Tenth, Thou shalt pray thy way into action.

Prayer is not a dead end. It is a temporary condition and usually a way to get back into the world. In short, praying is one way to move our hearts, minds and bodies toward the divine purpose in this life.

WHEN I DIE

"What happens when I die?" That's the most difficult question to answer and perhaps the most troubling for religious leaders. It often acts like a lightning rod, attracting all the anxiety of a lifetime.

Much of what religion says and does could arguably be classified as a response to this fundamental query, but before we get to the classic answers, it is important to recognize that all language about life after death is allegorical. It is describing what it might be like.

We have been promised by prophets and gurus (even by the son of God in one religious tradition) that there is an existence beyond the grave, but the vocabulary needed to describe it has not been invented. Word pictures and faith are all we have. We've described life after death as a time of eternal rest, days filled with sweetness and light, or a blank plane of bliss-filled nothingness. Some say it's like a mansion with many rooms or a great regal hall. Who knows what it will be like in reality?

I would suggest that three popular scenarios arise when exploring our journey beyond the grave. First, there are those who suggest there is nothing after death, and that we are no more than biological entities that suffer through a relatively brief time on earth and then perish. It is a rather harsh idea on first blush, but you have to admit that it makes you pause. Second, there is the commonly held idea of reincarnation. When you die, you are transmuted into another life form and return to earth This has been a very popular notion and has been around for several millennia, at least. Third, there is the notion that when we die we return to the God from whom we were made in the first place. By means of a general resurrection, a special day of judgment or a thousand-year rule, God appears as the final arbiter of justice who stands at the portal of eternal life separating the sheep from the goats, so to speak.

While there are many silly preoccupations in any religious tradition, their common fascination with peering behind the dark veil of death serves a very useful purpose. Trying to see past death helps us to live now. Think about it. There is a direct correlation between our theories of resurrection or reincarnation and how we structure our daily routine. The eternal disposition of our soul is like the little magnet we used to hold under iron filings when we were kids in school. It realigns all human activity. This is the measure I would hold up against any life-after-death theory. Does it motivate me to live well now, to respect the patterns of love and justice which are built into the created order?

A primary example of how a resurrection theory can corrupt our daily living is the Greek myth of the immortality of the soul. According to this Hellenistic mind set, the spiritual realm could not be defiled, while the embodied world was undeniably tainted. Therefore, when death occurred, it was argued that the fallen and corrupt body would naturally decompose, while the soul would live on forever. This is a pretty popular theory, but the problem is that it tends to make the time spent on earth look like punishment. Energy spent on caring for this planet or improving the livelihood of others was not seen to be worth much. It's not an exaggeration to suggest that the dominance of the theory of the immortality of the soul has led to a denigration of the natural order and the ecological crisis our world now faces.

So the question is vital: "What happens when I die?" We will be a sorry species when we stop asking it. The answer is equally important because it is on the basis of our response that we construct most of our life's hopes.

DOES GOD REALLY, REALLY EXIST? PROOF #3

When the mail arrived yesterday, it was maddening to see that the utilities bill was higher than usual. We try so hard to conserve water—flush the toilet less frequently, turn off taps and take short, crisp showers instead of long, deep baths. What was causing the increase? After scouting out the bathroom and laundry room, I found the culprit in the kitchen—a dripping faucet.

Looking at the guilty fixture, I was satisfied that I had found the real reason for my inflated bill. But on inspection, it was not actually the faucet, but a defective rubber washer inside that was not sitting properly in its place. After a few turns with a wrench, I realized that some parts had been put in backwards. How could the previous owner have been so foolish? Once I had reversed the error, I found that I hadn't solved the problem after all. It still dripped. Of course, it wasn't the washer itself, but the last renovation which was at fault. The old taps, which are easy to repair, had been replaced with the new single module variety—a handy person's nightmare. So it was the re-make of the kitchen that made my water bill go up, and that renovation was necessitated because the house was too small and needed the addition of a breakfast nook.

So, now I know. The real culprit, the cause of my dripping faucet, was the original builder, who made the house too small. But the house was made this way because of the economy of that era. People didn't have enough money to build bigger, and that state of affairs was caused by the economic depression which ended with the frugal war years. Ah ha! Now my dripping faucet was caused by World War II.

Of course, most historians would argue that World War II was not self-starting. It had many antecedent causes—greed, fascist animosity, ethnic hatred. These natural elements were mixed with the crushing vengeance of the Versailles Treaty, which was overly punitive toward the vanquished. So, in some sense, the Second World War was a direct result of the First and that great global conflict was, itself, a culmination of a host of interacting factors—a shift in the use and control of capital, the buildup of the arms race, the industrial revolution, the breakdown of European monarchies and revolutionary advances in military technologies.

All right. At last, I have come to the bottom of it all. I have a high water bill because of gun wielding revolutionaries from the nineteenth century who were overthrowing the evil empires which emerged from the late middle ages. But then when you think about it, these revolts were occasioned by the injustice of feudalism which, itself, was the brainchild of those people who struggled out from under the collapse of the Roman Empire.

Finally I have an answer. It was the greed and decay of Roman rulers which caused my dripping kitchen tap. I suppose this could go on forever, one thing leading to another, until I discover that my high water bill was caused by the first human beings to crawl out of a cave—but they themselves were not made from thin air. Someone created them and set them in motion. It's God, the Creator of the universe, who made all things — bright and beautiful, dark and ugly. Therefore, since God is the primary cause and first mover of all things, my utilities bill went over the top by action of the Almighty.

This reduction of all events to the first cause, to a Being that started it all, is known as the classical proof for the existence of God. If we trace any set of events backwards in time, we will finally come to original cause, the One who started it all.

This thinking is not unlike those theorists who claim that the universe began with a big bang; that the evidence of an ever-expanding universe points to an original instant in time when the whole thing was started by the explosion of a massive gas cloud. At the conception of all life, there had to be an instigator, an agent who began the process.

The beauty of this theory, whether the scientific or the religious, is that it ties all living beings together across time and space. In the sixties we sang, "No One Is an Island," and that lesson is becoming more and more clear to us. God and creation and human beings—we are all growing and evolving into a colossal co-creating community. Amen! Is it any wonder that I can return to my leaking faucet, indeed, to all my life's work, with a holy patience?

BEWARE OF VIRTUE

Hollywood is changing. A few years ago, they would have laughed at the idea of making a movie about religion and sin. This is not so any longer!

Have you seen "The Scarlet Letter?" Taken from an old yet classic novel of the same name written by Nathaniel Hawthorne, the plot revolves around the nature of human virtue and sinfulness. Strangely enough, apart from the typical happy-ever-after ending, the film directors stayed away from the obvious temptations of turning the story into a sex-crazed romp through 17th century puritanism. On the contrary; the scenes of sexual dalliance, which lead to accusations of adultery, are done with mythical artfulness, proving that you don't need nudity to produce sit-on-the-edge-of-your-sex-drive sensuality.

While I was taken by the passionate flavour of the tale, the scenery of the Maritimes, the haunting sound track, and the rock-hard loyalty and dedication of the heroine, Hester Prynne, it was the interplay between virtue and sin that took my breath away. In short, the movie makes abundantly clear that human beings are most dangerous when they think themselves to be most virtuous. The story lives out that old adage that the road to Hell is paved with good intentions.

The plot begins with a promising dream—to create a new world where the corruptions of state religion could be avoided. This land would be the site for the shimmering city of light mentioned in Matthew's gospel (Matthew 5:14). To achieve this good intent, the townsfolk of a small puritan establishment hold fast to their rules of order, beating down any hint of devilry with a resolute and ruthless hand. When a young couple, Hester and Arthur (the pastor) fall in love and lust, the town turns to gossip. When Hester becomes pregnant, they turn to spite, taking out the fury of their righteousness on the adulterous woman who refuses to give her lover's name. To expose the pastor would be to commit him to the gallows, so she keeps her secret stoically through all manner of emotional and physical deprivation. As punishment for her stubbornness, the elders of the community contrived a unique device. She must wear a scarlet "A" on her dress at all times to proclaim her sin to any who look upon her. It seemed like a just and fitting reward for her sin.

Whatever this film might say about the patriarchal bias of the Christian moral code or the abuse by clergy of their sacred relationship with parishioners, it is a stunning condemnation of "good" people trying to keep to their "good" principles.

There's nothing wrong with their moral standards. It seems both noble and desirable to protect the foundations of society from the erosive desires of individuals and to keep clear the professional boundaries of clerics. But when virtue is mixed with pietism, it is a potent concoction, and the movie makes this abundantly clear. The fervent beliefulness of the townspeople seduces them into equating their very human judgments with the thoughts and prerogatives of God. Claiming eternal significance for the laws of their fledgling village, they get caught in the spiral of witch-hunting where even small children are not exempt. Look out!

Moreover, there is a particular horror in puritan virtue gone amuck—whether of the 17th or 20th century. It often gets fixated on sexual indiscretions while completely ignoring the larger and often more destructive social evils. Let we who are religious beware. No matter how infallible we feel, no matter how clearly we may make our rules, they are fixed in time and space, and our God—whether Buddhist, Hindu, Muslim, Jewish or Christian—lives above and beyond our grasp. What the good people of Hester Prynne's day needed was a healthy serving of humility about their own virtue and a generous helping of compassion for the brokenness of others. Is that a message for our time?

THE HIDDEN GOD

Ever notice how God's not around just when you need her?

If the "Good Shepherd" had stood at your elbow, you might have stilled your tongue and avoided that hurtful scene with your mother. If an all-loving, heavenly Father had been the least bit interested in your well-being, you wouldn't be fighting lung cancer. Had the omnipotent Creator of all life been standing with you on the curb, you would have seen that car coming. Surely, the Eternal One could have whispered in our ear that the gun was loaded or that the road was icy.

Who hasn't known the sinking feeling of aloneness—that there is no guiding hand, no pre-programmed direction in this earthly existence? Feeling isolated and totally vulnerable, we cry out, "So, where are you God? Where are you when I need you?"

It's predictable that the complaint over God's apparent absence is voiced within the human heart, but it is quite surprising to hear the same concern echoed in scripture.

After all, we think of it as a "holy" book. Surely in its pages the mysteries of God's abiding presence are revealed.

Those unfamiliar with the bible or those who read it selectively may not recognize that a dominant experience of God is one of absence rather than presence. Time and again, when the hero or heroine turns around to get the helping hand of the Almighty, God slips from the scene. At first glance, it does seem strange that a text devoted to witnessing to God's saving acts should contain so many stories outlining God's lack of action. Nevertheless, a good deal of the biblical record explores the sensation of God's abandonment.

There is, of course, the Jonah tale in which a man laments how he was deserted by God and left to rot for three days inside a whale. Where was God when he needed him? In a similar fashion Jesus complains that it is at that very moment when his need is greatest, God abandons him—leaving him literally hanging. David, Sarah, Abraham, Peter, Moses, Mary, Martha—they all knew how thundering God's silence could be.

But abandonment is not the final word, for there is a twist in scripture. According to the Bible, God's absence is not a matter of time and space so much as a matter of perception. When we look at the biblical narrative, as dramatic as God's absence may be, God's hidden presence is equally startling. In her old age, Sarah was astounded by God being with her in the birth of a child. Likewise, the two travellers on the road to Emmaus were stunned when the stranger they met on the road, the one who sets their hearts on fire, turned out to be Jesus. In one parable, the absent God was actually present in the form of a lost prisoner, a naked waif or a thirsty outcast.

To use contemporary images, God is hidden in the beggar sleeping on the subway vent or an AIDS sufferer seeking healing or the abused child running for safety. When you meet a bag lady on the street, that is God asking you for some spare change. Standing by the bedside of a rape victim, you are looking down into the eyes of God's pain.

The bible's ironic final message is that God is often present precisely when we sense his absence. It's just that we don't have the eyes to see her for she appears in a form other than the Mighty Warrior King. Often God is revealed in a still small voice of comfort, in the struggle for survival, or in the challenge for justice. So if you are wondering where God is to be found, you may have to look into the cracks and corners of your life, exactly where any self-respecting deity shouldn't be. Miracles of miracles, God may then appear.

I BELIEVE

"It must be discouraging to belong to a church that doesn't believe in anything anymore—not even in God!" The letter ended with an exclamation point.

My thoughts skipped a beat. What do I believe anyway? Have I been so critical of religion that I can no longer wring even a half-hearted conviction out of my faith tradition? I wasn't sure how to respond to my correspondent. It would be rash to suggest that my religion has no "fundamental" principles, but the classic expressions of belief no longer seem to speak to me convincingly. However, I'm certainly not giving up on God. So here, my friend, is what I believe. It begins and ends, as all faith statements must, with the necessity of trusting.

> I trust that I am not alone.
> I trust that the Creator of Life will meet me
> in the here and now.
> I trust that the God who speaks to this world
> will call us to love and justice.
> I trust that in all our laughter and tears, we
> hear the echo of God's pain.

If that quick sketch is not enough, I'll elaborate.

First, I believe there is more to life than meets the eye. Before our birth, we were joined to the source of all life, hard-wired into the mainframe, so to speak. Being at one with the universe, we had no sensation of isolation. But once we are born, we become separate and know ourselves to be detached. It is not surprising that we spend our lives striving to regain the unity we once knew. While everyone feels alone, even alienated from others, we also sense that existence is not a random event. There are cycles to the seasons and patterns to the living and dying of all things. These rhythms are the footprints of a Maker. God is close as breath, as regular and dependable as a sunrise.

Second, I do not experience this God as a neutral proposition nor an indifferent hypothesis. I can't pray to an idea. I believe God is an encounter, an embodied presence which yearns to be lived out on earth. In the gracious words of a friend, in the loving touch of a partner, in the search for just relationships, and in the struggle for a world free of violence, God meets and talks to us, urging us to respond. There is no time nor space more sacred than any other. Every waking moment is an opportunity for a rendezvous with the eternal.

Third, having been shaped from the life-force of the universe, human beings are made for living and loving. It comes naturally. Of course, we are able to turn this prime directive into twisted purposes—control, abuse, injury and torture. Indeed, we can be sharp-fanged beasts. But as beings who come from the source of all life, we have an instinct for justice—to find and preserve the equilibrium where all people can have the opportunities and necessities for a good and decent life.

Finally, you've probably guessed that I don't pray to a sky-god who lives in the "sweet by and by." I take no comfort in a heaven that is distinct from this earth. At this point in my life, I believe God is found down here in the muck and confusion, at all our parties and wakes. And when we journey through the valley of the shadow, our Maker walks and weeps beside us—not as spiritual superhero, but as a friend who is just as taken aback by the suffering in our lives as we are.

That's it in an 800-word nutshell. It may seem hard to credit, but these few lines have taken hours to craft because I am exploring the pathways of the heart that do not open up easily to the workings of the mind. Nonetheless, here they are.

6 GOD LOVES A GOOD STORY

MAKE ROOM
FOR MYTH

There is a wonderful story about Martin Luther, the founder of Protestantism, and his dedication to the mythic side of the religious life. (Who knows if it actually happened?) In a gesture to protect his fledgling movement, he met with another Christian reformer named Ulrich Zwingli, a Swiss Protestant of another stripe. They met in the German village of Marburg to negotiate 15 key principles on which all of their followers could agree. Debating around the clock in several shifts, they achieved an incredible consensus agreeing upon 14 standards of the faith.

The stumbling block came with the 15th issue. Once the priest pronounced the words of consecration, was Christ actually present in the bread and wine of the Eucharist? With worlds hanging in the balance and the entire safety of the Reform movement at stake, Zwingli and Luther could not agree over this final point. The Swiss delegation read the words of institution contained in the gospels, Hoc est corpus meum, (translated literally as "this is my body") and understood Jesus to be saying that the bread and the wine are symbols. Zwingli was a modern man after all. He knew that bread was just flour, yeast and water. There was no divinity in it!

Martin Luther is reported to have written the same words, Hoc est corpus meum, on the table in chalk. Whenever the discussion turned to the issue of the sacrament of communion, he pointed to his scratching and declared that Jesus meant what he said. Luther argued, as any good medieval scholar would, that finite matter was capable of containing the infinite. In his mind, the loaf was much more than physical matter. It was fellowship, trust, justice, compassion and love all rolled into one. You could hardly break bread with another and not feel the abiding presence of the divine spirit.

Luther was right! When we break a loaf of bread, we recall the many shared meals of the past. We recognize that we are participating in a ritual of communion where we learn trust and mutual respect. The loaf embodies our best aspirations for a whole and well-fed community. It contains the best of our dreams for the future.

Zwingli's modern 20-20 vision, which boasts about its accuracy, has been blind. There is more to life than meets the eye. Human beings do not live by what they see. Contrary to all expectations, we make most of our big decisions on the basis of what lies hidden behind the external reality. In fact, myth is as vital to us as air or water.

This may sound ridiculous, but pause for a moment and reflect on the great moments in your life. When you fell in love, was it the empirical data about the other which captured your heart—the shape of his nose, the size of her eyes? These are just the surface issues and very quickly ignored. Our hearts are moved by the spirit and promise that a relationship represents. Similarly, how many people really tally up the impressive facts about an automobile and then dispassionately make a choice for one or another? Prior to all the calculations, we have established our own self-image—seeing ourselves seated in a particular vehicle, relishing what this image represents. The final purchase is confirmation of what we have already come to believe about ourselves.

Call it romance or mystery or intuition. Whatever the title, we live by the mythic images of what could be, and we organize reality to conform to these powerful principles. Myth directs our actions, soothes our hungry souls and draws us forward into greater achievements of wisdom and courage.

When the myth dies, life is flat and tasteless—like bread without salt and yeast. Whether we are believers or not—Jewish, Christian, Muslim, Hindu or Buddhist—Luther has a word of wisdom. Let us not forget the mystery in living. It is more than you can taste or see or feel—and it is in all that we taste and see and feel.

DANDELIONS AND DAILY LIFE

If you had passed by my house this morning, you would have seen me on my hands and knees plucking, pulling and pruning the dandelions in the front lawn. It was 6:35 a.m., and while my partner was working busily beside me, I could feel her scepticism. "What's the point? They're flowers, after all. God created them for beauty. Why dig them up and why at such an ungodly hour?" Why indeed?

It's quite simple. I hate dandelions! They mess up the neat symmetry of my carefully manicured edges. The rank-on-rank even cut of the grass is disrupted and corrupted by all the sneaky dandelion shoots which push head and shoulders above all else. They're so visible. Much like dirty laundry, these little yellow flowers are a stain on my reputation.

Walking about the neighbourhood in the morning, I am struck by the many finely clipped, putting-green lawns which surround so many homes. A tremendous amount of effort has gone into nurturing that clean, crisp luscious look. There's not a stray yellow flower in sight. Take enough strolls about town, and you begin to assume that grass was meant to grow free of intrusions. Weeds are a blight, an abnormality. Dandelions are a pestilence, an abomination, dare I say it—a sin. I think I must be developing a "dandelphobic" attitude.

I wasn't always this distressed over weeds. In fact, in past incarnations, dandelions caused not a stir in my heart or mind. Previous houses which I owned have been literally besieged by the little delicacies, and I didn't flinch. "Let them grow," I would say. "They're cheaper than buying perennials at the garden centre." But ... being surrounded by clean lawn experts, I feel obliged to change my ways, to accept the sad reality that dandelions are a god-forsaken weed deserving to be dug up or gassed out. It's only natural.

Stop! Stop right there and re-read those opening paragraphs. Look at what is happening to my thinking. I have taken a normal occurrence—a growing flower, transmuted it into a problem, accepted the implicit values of my society and fabricated a principle around what is natural. The final step in this chain of thought is to destroy the troublesome exception to my rule.

Most gardeners, when we are sober and away from our lawns, will admit that dandelions are not inherently evil or abnormal. They are just a persistent plant. Stretch the point a bit, and we might even concede that they are a gift of God. You can use them in salads. They will even produce a respectable wine if handled properly.

Human beings have always developed theories around what is "natural." It's part of the struggle for clarity and assurance, and while this categorizing of life's events into natural and unnatural is often a necessary step in the evolution of thought, it is also a trap. We can find ourselves caught believing that our categories and principles have lasting significance, that the world is actually created on the basis of some very finite theories. We start to pretend that nature is what we make it. How foolish and dangerous! There is no celestial record book which lists dandelions under a category of "weed." That's something we have decided. The "natural" is a human construct.

Looking at the pile of uprooted dandelions, I was reminded of many other instances when human beings have destroyed what they thought was "unnatural." During the Nazi regime in Europe, Jews, communists and homosexuals were considered to be expendable, deserving of destruction precisely because they were contrary to the order of nature. A similar fate awaited black slaves who were brought to this continent while the aboriginal peoples of this land were slaughtered and oppressed as a subnormal species. For many centuries women were considered by the church to be naturally inferior and so subjected to a multitude of abuses.

How misleading and frightening are our categories! Racism, sexism, homophobia are essentially the result of human paranoia mixed with self-righteousness. Often they also employ some theory of "natural order" as their justification for violence and vitriol against vulnerable minorities. One check against the rise of prejudice in an increasingly mean-spirited world is a healthy humility about our human categories. They may not be as eternal as we imagine. Maybe that's why God created dandelions—to inspire in us a more gracious tolerance and wisdom.

FORGIVENESS HURTS Last week I heard a parable which spoke volumes about the pain of forgiveness. There once was an aged father, Pedro, who was estranged from his beloved and only son, Pablo. It had begun as an innocent disagreement fought across the generation gap. Pablo had borrowed his father's prized wrist watch so he could wear it on a date. Unfortunately the family heirloom was lost. The father was furious, the son unrepentant. As the years passed this small misdemeanour festered and infected their relationship. Pedro and Pablo found it harder and harder to meet eye-to-eye, to crack the smiles that would bring about reconciliation. Eventually, they gave up in frustration. The chasm that separated them had grown too deep. Pedro blamed his son for his self serving and wasteful lifestyle — single-minded egotist! Pablo detested his father's mean-spirited accusations — unyielding grouch! Years passed. They drifted apart and lost touch.

Now nearing the end of his life, stricken with cancer, Pedro longed to be reunited with his son. The old arguments seemed trivial when viewed from the exit door of this life. What was a silly watch when life itself was ticking away all too rapidly? He wanted to see his boy at least once more, to ask and offer forgiveness. Unfortunately, the father had no idea of son's whereabouts. It would have been over a decade since they even corresponded. His last letter was returned with "address unknown" printed neatly across his son's name. Where to begin? Pedro combed the countryside, checked old friends and asked family members. The general consensus was that the wayward son was in the region of Madrid, but no one could say exactly where.

Desperate, Pedro took out an ad in the "personals" column of the city newspaper. It was a simple, direct plea. "Pablo, my son, where are you? I am dying. All is forgiven. Meet me on the steps of city hall next Saturday morning— I just want to say good-bye. Your Father." Saturday morning arrived and rounding the corner of the city hall you can imagine Pedro's surprise to find 837 Pablo's on the front steps of city hall, all waiting to meet their long-lost, and now-forgiving father.

The prodigal son, the prodigal father, they live in great bunches in our world, don't they? There are so many people longing for, lining up for their share of forgiveness. How strange that it is painful, both to give and receive. It is painful to offer forgiveness since it requires a bold assessment of our role in injustice. Rather than ignoring the sticks and stones that have broken our bones and our souls, forgiveness begins when we admit that we have been wronged. "I am hurt." "You have treated me poorly." Until these phrases can be uttered, the injustice named clearly, there can be no hope of giving forgiveness. Often, the naming means reliving the injury, and it may seem easier to suppress it. It requires a good deal of self confidence to confront some wounds others have inflicted upon us and an equal measure of courage to confront the culpable parties honestly.

Forgiveness is painful to receive too. Just as with the offering, so also in the receiving of forgiveness, injustice must be acknowledged before true reconciliation can begin. We who have wronged another must face squarely our inappropriate deeds, know them for our own and find the humility to depend upon another person's trust and graciousness. Only then can we receive some respite from our regret and guilt.

Whether in giving or receiving, forgiveness requires trust. That's the rub. There are times when trust is impossible. The bridges have been burned. All too often organized religion has forced forgiveness, ignoring the brokenness, the shattered trust, the unwillingness to recognize the hurt that has been caused. This is a grave error, for human beings are not infinitely expansive. At times they break and can't be put back together.

Forgiveness cannot be forced like a commandment. It is not an imperative. Rather, forgiveness is an indicative. It arises out of a genuine invitation. People can't extract it from you, and that means that it may never happen. Abused children may never find it in their hearts to forgive. Battered women, employees without work may not be able to offer any forgiveness to those who have harmed them. That's one of those rough edges of human life. In the end, forgiveness is a miracle. We can only await for it to happen. For all the Pablos and Pedros of the world, I hope the miracle comes. Patience and hope will have to suffice in the meantime.

A RANDOM ACT
OF KINDNESS

In the bleak and bitter months, when the dark shroud of our northern twilight is lifting from our daily lives (at a rate of four minutes a day I am told), we all need a ray of light, a reason to hope that the frost does not have the final word. Spring is on its way. Here is my piece of sunshine. It comes as a down-home story, a random act of kindness which proves beyond a shadow of a doubt that human beings are still capable of great trust and compassion, even in the lean and mean '90s.

My tale begins with Pam, a single mother living on the edge of survival. She's dying. It was a shock at first, but now we've known for almost a year. At a glance, she doesn't look all that sick, but her pancreas will literally shut down ... soon. Vomiting, nausea and tiredness have dogged her waking hours. The doctor gave her six months to a year, with no miracle cure in sight, no reprieve.

Running on the outside of the medical predictions, Pam tidied up her affairs. She made a video tape for her only son, trying to impress on him how much she loves him and cares about his future. She arranged with friends to conduct a fitting farewell, allocated her furniture to various friends and made her peace with the extended family. It's a dreary, desperate business, looking straight into the abyss, trying not to flinch.

As the summer drew on, Pam told me her time was short and all the dreams of her youth looked impossible. She'd never had a lot of money or opportunity. Now there would be no great trip to Disney World. She will not see her son graduate from high school, something she hadn't been able to accomplish, but he could. No flashy car would grace her driveway. Likewise the quiet retreat in the country was out of reach. Pam's one secret passion, only whispered to a kindred spirit in the nighttime of her fears, was to drive a blue mustang convertible. That was clearly out of the question now.

Fall brought chill weather and Pam's world closed in. She had fewer good days than bad. One morning when hope was waning, she heard a car honking in the driveway. "Silly people, to make so much noise."

Looking out through the curtains, she spied a blue streak in the fog outside. Loaded with a gang of friends come for a visit, there sat a blue mustang convertible, the latest model no less. In a I-don't-believe-my-eyes shuffle, Pam made her way to curb, were she was informed that the whole company was travelling out of town—to see the sights and have lunch in a quaint little inn. It was their treat! And no one was driving the car but Pam. Her hidden wish had driven up to her front door, white leather seats and all. What a gift! There was never one more precious.

Pam was living her life moment by moment and in that day she certainly filled a lifetime of memories. Running into the house she dug out her Elvis Presley photo and stuck "the King" on the dash as mascot. Then came the photo session. You could almost read the captions of her dreams looking at her souvenir pictures. "Lounging Woman Relaxes in Driver's Seat of Blue Ford

Mustang." "Pam Sits on Hood of New Car in a Suggestive Pose." "Wild Ride through the Country." "Top Speed Companionship."

It was a glorious day. Even the chill winds couldn't dampen their spirits. Keeping the top down in rain or shine, through night and day, they rode around until the tank ran out of gas and Pam ran out of energy. Wonderful friends, wonderful laughs. Wonderful...

It all happened because Pam's soul mate, hearing her dream, had approached the local Ford dealership. Explaining Pam's state of health and her secret fantasy, she asked if it was possible to let her dying friend have a test drive even though she wouldn't ever be able to buy a blue mustang convertible. The understanding dealer handed over the keys and said, "Here, take it for the day and have a good time."

Miracles still happen. Awaiting spring, I live for these random acts of kindness which burst upon existence, fresh and fragrant. What else is life made for?

REMEMBERING AND COMPASSION

We all have an Aunt Edna. She lives in the senior's complex over town, has that sit-around-the-fire grandmotherly charm and, as of late, she's losing her mind. Actually, it's not really her mind that is deteriorating, just her memory.

My Aunt Edna is dignity personified. In younger years, she would never set foot outside her door in anything but the latest fashion. Dressed to the nines with none of this polyester and pearls, my aunt looked her "Paris collection" best at all times.

You can imagine my dismay when her memory loss became serious. There was the time she called the house in a breathless fluster. "I can't remember where I put my teeth." Edna had replaced the real ones with a set of dentures—a great blow.

I asked the obvious question: "Where did you put them last?" Talking her through the apartment, she scouted out the bathroom and her night stand by the bed. "They're not in the glass." A search of the kitchen counter was equally fruitless.

In desperation I asked her to recall what she was doing just before she missed them. "I was eating a sticky bun, but I didn't like it. They make them so sweet these days. I threw the whole thing out." A light blinks on. "Say Aunt Edna," trying to sound nonchalant, "Why don't you look in the kitchen garbage can." Sure enough, there were her false teeth still stuck to the half-eaten chelsea roll. Still wedged in the dough, they went into the wastebasket along with the bun and she hadn't even noticed.

That's sad but not nearly as tragic as the time she came to the door not remembering what to wear. My knock caught her between bath and clothes closet. She knew she should do something, but had no memory of what exactly was needed. So she opened the door with a towel around her neck and a smile—nothing else. My heart sank for her lost dignity—how could the loss of memory loss be so cruel to a woman who wore her self-respect with such poise and class. When we forget, we do embarrassing, undignified things.

In the days when our nation contemplates war, when we gather around the cenotaphs in a thousand towns and cities, this country comes as close as it ever will to being holy. Cultivating our collective memory of past conflicts, the sacrifices it exacts, the hardships it imposes, is a very, nay essential, spiritual exercise. We recall faces of lovers, friends and family and remind ourselves that these people gave us the time that is now.

But they gave us much more. In remembering we inherit their spirit and give it birth. Their laments and laughter echo in our own, their hopes and visions come alive as we dream our dreams.

Now, as I walk past the war memorials, I shiver. Not from the cold, but from what seems to be a growing cultural amnesia. We have forgotten what made this country great—the intentional compassion of social safety nets: adequate medical care for all, assistance in times of unemployment, tolerance for those strangers at our kitchen door.

In a mad dash to slash budgets, we're a bit like my Aunt Edna. Forgetful and naked, stripped of the common sense benevolence which marked the Canada that so many have sacrificed to preserve.

Pity! My Aunt Edna looked so much better with all her clothes on!

SOMETIMES LOVE IS TOO MUCH

Can love hurt? There was a time when I thought violence was the singular result of anger and hate and greed—all those dark passions. While on the surface this seems usually to be the case, I have encountered those people for whom violence is a manifestation of something else, something deeper and more subtle, a state of heart and mind which presents itself—don't laugh—as virtue, even love.

Allow me to introduce Peter. He's a young man, medium build, twinkling eyes and pleasing manner. At first glance, he's the sort of kid I'd like my daughter to date. I met Peter while speaking about dating violence to the high school students. Here's his story.

"I am sixteen years old and I've never been in a girl's washroom before—not surprising since I'm a guy. But here I am, looking like the perfect idiot, holding the battered door I tore off the stall where my ex-girlfriend was hiding. Crazy . . . right?

"Let's get one thing straight. I'm not violent—really I'm not! You have to believe that, or you won't understand what I have to say.

"Looking around, watching this scene as if I were a surveillance camera in the corner of the john, I frown and I wonder how I got here. How did it all begin—the rage inside—the blind stampeding after the fleeing figure of my girl—the wrenching gut?

"You see, I love June—that's my girl . . . well that was my girl. I guess she's not speaking to me any more. Her parents want to press charges. They say I'm no good, a threat. Something about sexual harassment or assault. I only grabbed her shoulder once. Since when is that assault?

"Let me take it from the top. June and I have . . . had been going out for a few months. It was really great. I mean something special—like the movies. We had it all! I am so in love it is unbelievable—how we stick to each other, rush out after class to talk and walk together every spare moment we have. There is no time for anything else—all that matters is June.

"Then she asked me if she could go out with Roger, some little twerp from across town. 'Just for a date. Nothing serious! Only to talk and maybe have a drink together.' Nothing serious? You could have stuck me with a knife and hurt me less. How could my girl want to go out with some other guy? Wasn't I good enough? Didn't I love her enough? Couldn't I give her all she needed?

"Well we straightened that out right quick. She saw my point and that was the end of it. No open relationships with me! When you're mine, you're mine—all the way.

"Everything was cool. We had each other or at least that's what I thought until one of my spare periods when I saw her walking with Roger—the no-mind from the other side of tracks.

"I couldn't believe it. How could she do this to me, I mean to us?

"Well, I may be dumb and I may not have a lot of money, but I'm a straight-shooting dude. So I went right over to her, pushed them apart and started to ask her what was coming down. She said something about breaking up and me being creepy. I was stunned. That's when I grabbed her. Not hard—just enough to make her stay. She took off anyway and I didn't see her for a few days. She stayed away from me. So I waited for her after school—walked by her house—wanting to catch her alone—just to talk.

"Then this morning I saw her running into the school and I went after her calling for her to stop. Knots! My stomach was tied in a million of 'em. My head was pounding. I was out of breath and ready to throw up, all at once. As I followed her my mind kept asking, 'How could she? How could she? Doesn't she know how much I love her and need her'?

"By the time I got inside, she was already talking to some friends and pointing in my direction.

"That's when I lost it. I only wanted to make her listen, make her understand. She broke from the group and headed into the girls' washroom—thought she was safe I guess. But I ran right in after her. I just wanted to talk—nothing else. Nothing else mattered.

"When she locked herself in the stall, everything went berserk. I was shouting and smashing on the door. Now, here it is in my hands and she's gone.

"I'm not violent. I would never hurt her, I love her too much. Really, I do!"

The extent and severity of violence and abuse among teenagers is just now coming to light. What used to be called teasing or child's play is serious business to those who are victimized and almost everyone wishes it would stop. Equally frightening is the extent to which men are oblivious to their unwarranted and injurious behaviour. If the violence against young women is to cease, it can only happen when young men, like Peter, start to recognize their actions as abusive, controlling and degrading.

Peter's problem, and it is shared by many men in our community, is that often we don't know—we are unwilling to acknowledge—how inappropriate behaviour actually can become. We think we're just acting out our love for someone—the highest of virtues. How can love hurt? We are unable to recognize when have we crossed the line from exaggerated teasing and attentiveness, to unwarranted injury or violation.

To Peter, and all men in relationships who wonder about their behaviour, here is one guiding principle. Think of abuse as the dark side of love—love's violence. When that voice inside says "I need this person desperately—I'll die without her," we should be wary. What may appear to be the quintessential tenor of love according to Hollywood standards—an unblemished, all-consuming passion—may well be the beginning of addictive and possibly violent behaviour. That love which is "needed" to fill up the emptiness we feel inside, that love which cannot tolerate a certain level of ambiguity, nor muster a modicum of tolerance, is well on its way to becoming destructive.

There's a song lyric which runs "Sometimes love just ain't enough." Well, there are also times it can be too much.

THAT'S NOT WHAT I SAID

"That's not what I said!" How often do we protest that our words have been misinterpreted? A partner, friend or lover just doesn't seem to hear us clearly. It's a common complaint and a frequent excuse for ending a relationship. When the dust settles, we wonder how we could have said it differently. How to really communicate—-that's the question.

Some years ago, I was bouncing down a lonely stretch of highway in the back of a well-travelled jeep. A poor excuse for a rescue mission, we had just picked up three small children who had lived as "abandonados"—deserted kids—on the streets of San Jose, Costa Rica. The city had thousands of them, and under government supervision, my small party was bringing a few desperate ones to their first real home in a newly constructed village. At the end of our journey, foster parents and a welcoming community awaited.

The wind whipped in at all corners as we sat crouched in the back seat, little Maria on my lap. The darting eyes and guarded smile spoke of terror. I wanted to soothe her fears. Life was about to bless her with one of its miracles, but I was tongue-tied and nervous. Having just arrived in this foreign land, Maria was my first encounter with an authentic Spanish speaking person. Prior to this, Spanish had been little more than a lifeless classroom dictation lesson.

Holding this dark-haired wonder, I realized, with some amazement, that she didn't come with translation aids. No first-year charts of verbs, no cheat sheet at the back of the book, no helpful teacher to correct me—this is real life. What to say?

I took a stab at it and said, "You have such wonderful curls in your hair."

That produced a smile and a faint titter. Not much— just a squeak, but I felt her body relax ever so slightly. Leaning back in my arms as she watched the country roll by, Maria had accepted my offer of friendship. My mission accomplished, the delicate task of translation had worked—or so I thought.

It was only after we had deposited Maria in her new home and watched her melt into the warmth of caring parents, that the driver of the jeep told me what I had actually said. No matter what I thought my words conveyed, what she actually heard was, "My, what large mattresses you have in your brain."

It was a simple mistake. That's how I comforted my bruised ego; it was merely a matter of mixing up a few vowels and choosing a couple of bizarre words. But it makes a world of difference to Maria whether she has curls or mattresses and whether they're on her head or in her brain. It was at that moment that I realized translation is a tricky business. My intentions were good, but my skill was marginal and the end result was comical. I was lucky. Conversing with a small Spanish speaking child was a challenge, but it was nothing compared to the snarls of translation which have confounded human relationships even when we speak the same language. In all sorts of relationships, the outcome of miscommunication can be tragic and hurtful. How many have been broken on the sharp rocks of "that's not what I said?"

After years of doing counselling, I am convinced that three things are necessary for a faithful resolution of our interpersonal communication: humility, patience and trust. Humility teaches us that we do not have all the right answers—no one does. At best, human beings must grope towards truth through mutual assistance, knowing that we won't always get it right.

Patience keeps my tongue in check. Rather than blurt out well-worn, angry slogans, all parties must try to hear their inner spirit speaking. Listen for the hurts and hopes that lie behind our well-formed sentences. The real message is often hiding between the lines. Trust is perhaps the most difficult emotion to muster. When partners discuss separating, trust is stretched to the limit. Unfortunately, the very prospect of ending the relationship is enough to turn faithfulness into anger and confidence into mistrust.

Of these three ingredients, I am most often pleading for trust. There is no other bridge to healthy communion than believing in the virtues of the other side. No matter what the nature or outcome of our relationships, life is not about annihilating each other, proving our point at all costs or deliberately misconstruing "their" words.

Maria taught me that in spite of our words, miracle of miracles, with a little trust and love, we are still able to communicate.

WILL YOUR ANCHOR HOLD IN THE STORMS OF LIFE?

There is an old Methodist hymn that begins: "Will your anchor hold in the storms of life?" We sang it often enough as children and loved it even though in southwestern Ontario we had never seen an anchor nor ever needed something so weighty to hold us down in the storms that crossed our countryside. Last week, the lyrics came to life as I heard the tale of crossing the Queen Charlotte Sound, a body of water between the northeast tip of Vancouver Island and the coast of British Columbia. It's a particularly treacherous stretch of sea.

Like a funnel, it channels the water from the Pacific Ocean down a rather narrow 40-mile-wide passage. Swirling around three or four small island groups, with their hidden shoals that wait like needles to puncture an unsuspecting hull, it's every sailor's nightmare. With the full force of the ocean bearing down upon any hapless vessel, it has been the graveyard of many ships and their crews. When the tides are running high, you could hardly find a more difficult passage on the West Coast. So when the squalls are raging, small craft, sailboats and motor launches, wanting to pass from the island to the mainland's inside passage, must wait for seasonable weather—and there is one place you can wait it out. In a smallish bit of land just off the tip of Vancouver Island, there is a tiny haven—quite literally a harbour from the storm—and it's called God's Pocket.

Finally, I've been given a real-life parable to match the hymn I sang so lustily as a boy! There's something quite real about these geographical details that match the images conjured up by the hymn. When we run to God for safety from the torments of our lives—the death of a child, the loss of a job, the crisis in a relationship—we're seeking protection and a strategic rest. No matter how strong we might be, we all need that protective harbour, the anchor that will hold.

Of course, there are some folk who would turn their religious practice into a habitual haven. In prayer or praise, they hide from the waves of doubt or pretend that the waters of daily living are smooth as glass. Abdicating responsibility for their life choices, they regress into a childhood fantasy where there is no hurt or pain and a parent-god in the sky will make all their decisions for them.

The use of religion in this way is foolish, for every life must face its own storms, and God is not meant to be an escape from the harshness of living. God will not be used as an avoidance of life's tempests but only as a steadfast ally. Eventually, we have to venture out of the safe anchorage and try our sails.

Human growth is only possible if we cross the seas of maturity. Would that it were otherwise, but in order to become fully human, we will face dashed hopes and broken promises. No one gets to the other shore without being rubbed raw by the betrayal of a friend. Few of us will end our lives without knowing the devastation wrought by sickness and death. It isn't possible to be real and not know the weariness that makes us unable to accomplish what was once a simple task. Who won't feel the anguish of waiting for word from a loved one who is at a distance telling us that all will be well? Life is a journey through some pretty treacherous waters.

There's a piece of the story I didn't mention. Most people traversing Queen Charlotte Sound leave God's Pocket and head for the opposite shore for Safety Cove— which is on Calvert Island. And that's my point! Life is the constant passage across rough seas—it is the venturing out from one haven, risking the gales and reaching the safety of another.

The same is also true if you want to reach God's domain. You have to leave safety behind and take a chance on the channel. Now even a land-locked sailor like myself can understand that.

7 RELIGION AND POLITICS

IT'S OUR TURN TO TALK ABOUT LOVE

Once again, Canadians can take pride in the fact the United Nations has reported that for the third year in a row our country has been voted the most desirable country in the world in which to live. We might also recognize that right behind Australia, this land is regarded by the World Bank as the richest on the planet when our human and physical assets are tallied up. These are two pretty good reasons to be proud.

We can think of others—the grandeur of our mountains, the purity of our rivers, the breadth of our plains. Are we not good at lobster fishing, prairie farming and potato picking? All this is true.

But have you ever thought of Canada as a country of lovers? I know some starry-eyed souls would argue that the Mediterranean countries have this front covered. But what if we were lovers of a different stripe? What if we thought of love not just as a question of erotic affection and moonlight romance? Deep love can also be shared between neighbours and friends. It has as much to do with boundaries as with beds and is equally responsive to compassion as passion. What if we were a country filled with the kind of love that expressed itself through tolerance of our differences and in solidarity with the outcast?

Strange as it may seem, our brothers and sisters from Quebec have set a precedent for that style of loving. You may have heard the melody or caught the lyrics to the now famous unofficial "national anthem" of Quebec. It has fired the imagination of that people's cultural renaissance and is so respected and revered that it is now used as the traditional birthday song. Entitled "People of this Land," the chorus goes like this:

> Gens du pays, c'est votre tour,
> de vous laissez parler d'amour,
> Gens du pays, c'est votre tour,
> de vous laissez parler d'amour.

The same line repeated twice is translated as: "People of this land, it's your turn to speak about love." The verse is just as poetic: "The time that it takes to say, 'I love you,' is all that is left to us at the end of our days. The words that we speak, the flowers that we plant, are the only harvest we reap in the great garden of passing time."

Of course, it can be used as a powerful rallying cry for the cause of independence, but it is also a very moving statement of national purpose. In the context of global strife where the rabid jingoism of ethnic animosity is shredding the fabric of human compassion, what a novel, gentle approach to national identity! Have we not been the sensible northern country that sees our closest cousins as friends rather than foes? Have we not built a solid reputation as peacekeepers—the closest you could get to being collective or political lovers? Surely, our quest—yet to be fulfilled but nevertheless still alive—for a decent society which meets the basic needs of its citizens is a remarkable act of love.

There is a parable told of a famous rabbi who was known for his wisdom and wit. Once, two of his many disciples appeared with a question they felt would challenge the master's mind. "Rabbi do you know," they asked in excited tones, "when can we tell that darkness is turning to light? Is it when we can see the difference between a sheep and a goat? Is the night finally over when we can distinguish a thistle from a rose?" The rabbi looked at their earnest faces and replied: "You will know that a new day is dawning when you can look into the eyes of a stranger and see your brother or sister staring back."

May it be said of Canadians that we are lovers who recognize our brother or sister in every stranger we meet.

IT SEEMED LIKE A GOOD IDEA AT THE TIME

John was a young man during the '40s. Maybe that's why he put such trust in the old wise tales. Upon his arrival as the new schoolmaster in the windswept Saskatchewan village, the locals informed him that in the grasslands round about, there was an infestation of ticks. Little devils no bigger than a mustard seed would bury themselves in your skin to feed on your blood. Once bitten, the victim could suffer from the dreaded and fatal Rocky Mountain Spotted Fever. Given the hazard of the disease they carried, ticks were not to be taken lightly.

"Watch especially in your bed," they warned John.

"Ticks like dark warm places." But there was a remedy. "First, don't ignore them. And second, whatever you do, don't pull them out quickly." That would bring about sure disaster. Rather, it was suggested that when a tick was found buried in your skin, you should hold a match close to the spot. "The heat will cause the insect to let go of its fateful grip and back out of the hole it had dug in your skin."

Brilliant. Some old kitchen wisdom is, indeed, useful. Armed with this information, John went out to the small teacherage by the schoolhouse. Confident that he would be able to face down even the most stubborn of ticks, he slept well from Monday to Friday, without a single bite.

Then came his first close encounter. Waking at dawn on Saturday morning, he found a tick wedged into his thigh. Resolved, a tad overanxious, but unwilling to lose a moment's opportunity, John whipped out the matches and immediately began to heat the back side of the tick. Unfortunately, he was rather vigorous and indiscriminate in his application and not only singed his own skin but fried the legs off the tick. It was then unable to remove itself from his skin, even if it had wanted to. At that point, it was too late for John to do anything but squeeze the bug in its burrow and hope for the best. In the end, he suffered no ill effects, save for a slight inflammation of the thigh where the skin had been burned. Lucky John.

Isn't it strange how ethical and spiritual insights can arise? As I listened to his tale, I was drawn immediately into the predicament of the poor in this downsizing culture. They have been told for so long that they are parasites, people living off the life blood of others, biting into the healthy body of the economy with little regard for its survival.

The solution presented by many administrations, including most provincial governments, is to turn up the heat and make the marginalized squirm. By reducing benefits, cutting back on child care allowances, and squeezing the unemployed to work for low paying jobs, we're putting the flames to their feet and supposedly forcing people to crawl out of their parasitic dependence and fend for themselves. It works with ticks. Why not people?

What a spiritually bankrupt practice! The very measures intended to instill self-reliance among the disadvantaged are precisely the factors which make it impossible for them. When we penalize people for studying while they are on social assistance, or weaken the potential for good health through user fees, or reduce government services to marginal communities, or slash support systems to the disabled, we are making the cycle of poverty more difficult to leave, not easier. At the same time, we are destroying their dignity and soul, the essential sources of any self-renewal, and we end up with a lot of hungry people and burnt out communities.

As we, who put our trust in this "enlightened" policy of tough love, break our arms trying to slap ourselves on the back, the bread lines lengthen while the crimes induced by increased destitution threaten to swamp the neat social equilibrium we have established.

And just like John, having tried this quick and rather brutal fix to a problem that has taken a long time to create, sensitive citizens now find themselves in that precarious position of wondering if a much greater, potentially terminal calamity will strike us down. Will we be scorched by our own medicine?

Come to think of it, some kitchen wisdom is "old" precisely because it doesn't work.

THE PAINS OF CHARITY

The old adage declares that "it is better to give than receive." I would add that it is also much less painful. Anyone who has stood in a bread line will know that being on the receiving end of benevolence is no piece of cake. In fact, far from being uplifting, being the victim of charity is not a pleasant experience at all. It's soul destroying!

Unfortunately, as the North American world moves into a meaner and leaner 21st century, more and more people will have a first-hand taste of the bitter medicine we call "charity." Governments of all political stripes are selling off their welfare businesses, no longer seeing the physical and emotional well-being of their citizens as the domain of politics.

It has been the expectation of many provincial legislatures that as they pull back from their social programs, a

host of self-help groups, religious institutions and philan-
thropic organizations will pick up the slack. After all, they
say, these agencies traditionally shouldered the responsibility of caring for those who did not attract the attention
of law makers—the property-less, the job-less, the family-
less. Indeed, up until the middle of this century, all these
folk who were "less" were left to depend on the goodwill
of benevolence. On the surface, it seems to make sense to
return to the old ways. They worked once. So why not try
them again?

Contrary to this theory, charity has never been an
adequate structure for the support of the destitute.
Generous as North Americans are, willing as citizens may
be, there is a grave difference between state sponsored
social programs assisting the dispossessed and those pro-
vided by charitable agencies. Before we launch whole-
heartedly into divesting ourselves of our safety nets and
privatizing our societal compassion, it would be wise to
recognize the shortcomings of the charity-based models of
assistance and enumerate the pains it can cause.

Pain #1. Charity is not dependable. Charity is reliant
on the goodwill of the affluent and often dependent on the
emotional fads of the day. There are many times when
donated dollars do not arrive in the amounts necessary to
meet the need. How often, as a minister, did I run out of
benevolent money and discover that the food bank was
closed and the kitchen cupboard was bare? Those who
would cut government cheques, are you able to look into
the eyes of a desperate mother who has no milk for her

baby and say, "Sorry, we're all out of cash and food?"

Pain #2. Charity is arbitrary. Picture yourself on the street without enough money to survive. How can you predict or control the level of charitable assistance you might get from one agency to another? For instance, you might enter one church down the road that will give you a food basket only after you have taken Jesus into your heart as your Saviour and Lord. How easily our charity becomes an excuse for religious blackmail. And with a free market in benevolence, so to speak, who will control unjust practice? Who will call the soup kitchen to account if it gives out too little at Christmas? Is there a protection agency that polices food banks? Can anyone say to the not-for-profit housing project that they need to lower the rent?

Pain #3. Charity has a moral stigma. Unfortunately, it is still the case in our culture that to be without and dependent on the benevolence of others is to be considered sinful and less deserving of respect than those who are well-off. While it's punishment enough, this unspoken prejudice means that those who look or act in a morally "correct" manner will receive their charity quicker and in greater abundance than those who do not fit the accepted norms of our society.

Pain #4. Charity preserves the imbalance of society. Giving and receiving alms doesn't alter the fact that some people "have" while others do not. After the Christmas hamper is delivered, the rich are still rich and the poor are still poor. Give a person a free lunch and they will still need to come back for supper. Nothing is resolved. Quite the contrary, despondency is reinforced.

Pain #5. Charity is soul-destroying. The dependency created by benevolence, apart from its inadequacy as an agent of social transformation, eats away at the soul. Have you ever had to beg again and again? Have you ever had to hold out your hand to a stranger and plead for help because you can't provide for yourself or ask for bread for an underfed family? Very quickly your dignity is gone, the first casualty of poverty. It's difficult enough asking for your rights as they have been established by social charter; it's quite another order of humiliation when you must call upon the good graces of another for sustenance.

People of faith, I invite you to speak out. We are not engaged in merely a debate over societal structures or political expediency. Resisting the current attack on social programming is a battle for the preservation of souls. My God, let them not be sold out so cheaply!

WHY DO WE GAMBLE WHEN WE KNOW WE'LL LOSE?

When I was twelve, I learned a very important lesson from the penny arcade at the local carnival. Simple, really. When you gamble, you lose. You know the game. It looked like such a simple thing to toss the round hoop over the peg which held my prize (it was a little black watch, in this case). Five quarters and a dozen breathless attempts later, I was no closer to my goal—and I had, in the scant space of three minutes, wasted my entire day's fun money.

The family rules were strict on that score. All the kids received $1.25 for the day, and we could spend it however we decided. But once it was gone, there would be no further advances on the bank, no refunds for lost change. With pockets achingly empty, I spent the rest of the day watching my brother and sister enjoy themselves, eating hot ice-cream sandwiches and laughing at my foolishness: "Silly, everyone knows you can't win."

It was from that early lesson of hard knocks, rather than a religious fire and brimstone morality, which set me against gambling. And I have been wondering ever since why it is so popular. Could it be that the modern resurgence of gambling gives testimony to a greater spiritual malaise? Perhaps we're a hope-starved people. After a day on the shop floor pushing the same broom down the same aisle at minimum wage, a million dollar jackpot is the only possible source of expectancy. It's silly, it's impossible, but someday the 6/49 prize might just come home. Luck, good fortune, chance—they're the stuff of which dreams are made.

And make no mistake, human beings need hope as desperately as they need water and food. Without a vision, some reason to stretch beyond ourselves, people wither and die.

Perhaps North Americans gamble because life has become so predictable and boring. If we had the courage, we could look down the corridor of our lives and forecast most of our major and even minor decisions. Heavy-laden with the anchors of our mediocrity, we shuffle through our calculated lives. We long for a thrill, for the miraculous levity of surprise. There's something about the out-of-the-ordinary which lifts the drooping soul. Why should we be surprised by the popularity of games of chance that promise to break into the humdrum beat of living?

And finally, there are many people for whom gambling seems to be the only solution to an impossible situation. The bills run too high, and the cash flow runs too low. What is there to do but go for broke? Unfortunately, that is usually what happens.

In the end, my opposition to gambling is not based on a moralistic notion that games of chance are the devil's instruments. If you want a reason to hope, seek excitement or leave despair behind, gambling may be a legitimate solution for you. But I am disturbed if we begin to support the public purse (or the charitable one for that matter) by capitalizing on the spiritual and economic hunger of the wider society. Development through exploitation can only lead to more destructive and inappropriate cultures. When the community gambles, even with public support and encouragement, we all lose. I don't think the dynamics have changed much since that little fairground of my youth.

LAMENT FOR A NATION

When I was twelve, my favourite pastime was playing guns down in the valley behind the Dufferin Apartments. Each Saturday, Teddy Peas and I would form up teams and scatter into the woods. Many afternoons were spent in earnest pursuit of annihilating the "enemy." The one twist in our sport was that the "bad" guys were always the Americans. As the generation born immediately after the Second World War, it would have been more logical to choose the Japanese or the Germans as the ultimate danger, but it was not so.

Is this a parable of Canadian identity? All too often, Canadians define themselves negatively. "We're not like the United States." Rather than spend time examining our dis-ease towards the powerful empire south of the 49th parallel, it is more instructive to appreciate that a wild band of over-exercised boys in southern Ontario felt that there was something worth defending in this country. We were not sophisticated political pundits nor anthropological experts, yet we knew intuitively that Canada was worth preserving as a distinct land. It was a sacred space.

Thirty years later, I am struck with an even greater desire to defend a way of life and a society which defies being a cultural melting pot. As globalization and open markets threaten to level all cultural barriers, this land "made for you and me" is more sacrosanct than ever.

It is tragic that at the very point when a solidly Canadian identity is most desirable, I sense that our determination is weakening. Who will raise a lament for a nation which is selling its soul for economic security and political expediency? Surely, we can muster a list of reasons to preserve this small band of peoples clinging to its southern border? What makes this place holy?

First and foremost, Canadians have had a faith-filled appreciation for the collective good, being unimpressed with the hero-worshipping individualism of our friends to the south. Whether of aboriginal, Scottish, Ukrainian, French or Japanese extraction, we have been boringly constant in our protection of the underdogs and marginalized peoples. Unemployment insurance, old age security, comprehensive welfare and subsidized higher education are the benchmarks of our maturity as a nation. We have been, above all else, a people, not a loose collection of lone rangers.

Second, no matter how cold it is at Portage and Main or on the corner of St. Catherine and Peel, Canadians love the ruggedness of our climate. Under all the winter-time complaining, who doesn't detect a whiff of pride? "How high was the snowdrift?" "It was how many degrees below zero?" More than any other ideological principle or physical element, Canadians are shaped and bound together by our survival against the vicious winds and unrelenting storms that ravage this land. There is no need for an official policy of bilingualism, since we have a common language which bridges all tongues—we call it weather. Moreover, the omnipresent snow banks and black ice have given Canadians a scepticism over quick fixes, inflated promises and pretentious beliefulness. We have an uncanny, and ploddingly pedestrian attitude to life's major problems. Bragging is not suffered well. Surely, this is the reason for the respect we receive from both the peaceful and conflicted peoples we encounter abroad.

Third, we are struck with a common sense or a predilection for order and decency. People still line up patiently for everything from movies to micro-surgery. We have laws to protect the common decency and programs to ensure each person's health. With all its warts and problems, Medicare still stands as a great achievement of which most Canadians are rightfully proud.

Finally, we love our cultural heritages and cling to an impossible regional distinctiveness. Maritimers are wedded to their eastern shores, even when they live in Winnipeg. Westerners are the only sensible, risk-taking people left in the country. Quebecers have dutifully considered themselves a sovereign and separate nation for two centuries now. Newfoundland is still pondering if it wants to join the Dominion. Vancouverites behave like a separate and enlightened republic, while Ontarians complain of being milked by the have-not provinces. The aboriginal peoples claim sovereignty over vast sections of the country with great flourish. The territories are a frozen world cut off from the balmy southern climes. What an improbable, delightful patchwork of peoples. It should never hang together—and yet it does. This impossible possibility is the most miraculous, dare I say sacred, quality of Canada.

I make such a claim with a certain patriotic zeal, but

also cognizant of how much our country represents the present state of the world. Rising tribalism and ethnic animosity threaten to tear away any shred of collective commitment to the planet's common welfare. Hence, should the Canadian experiment die, whether by vivisection or a gradual dissolution into the American way of life, it would be a defeat of the human project. Who will raise a lament for this nation? Until we do, all the children's games in the world will not prevent the disappearance of a beautiful dream.

WALTZING MATILDA I'm never convinced that religion is only something which happens in church or synagogue. Last night while visiting with friends, I experienced it in a tavern. The band was playing down, lights were low, and someone called out for "Waltzing Matilda." It was only as I listened and had the tale of the song translated for me that I understood how theological issues crop up in the strangest places.

You probably know snatches of what must be close to the unofficial Australian national anthem. We sang "Waltzing Matilda" around the camp fire as children, didn't we? Apart from the doleful melody, which hinted at tragedy, the words were so foreign we probably didn't know what we were singing.

The song, reportedly written by a musician called Banjo Peterson, is about a swagman, the 19th century version of a street person, who was camped by the side of river (billabong). He's waiting for his pot (billy) to boil. Hungry and underfed, but free and unadorned (some critics argue this landless, resourceful hero is the archetype for the land down under), he watches as a stray sheep (jumbuck) comes down to the river to drink. The swaggie kills the sheep and hides it in his shopping cart (tucker bag). No sooner is the deed done, than the landed aristocrat (the squatter) comes along with three troopers to apprehend this vagrant. The swaggie jumps in the river and drowns himself rather than putting up with the maltreatment of the squatter. The chorus refrain echoes the plot: "Waltzing Matilda, Waltzing Matilda, you'll come a-Waltzing Matilda with me, and he sang as he sat and waited while his billy boiled, you'll come a-Waltzing Matilda with me."

The "Waltzing Matilda," which as a child I assumed was a vague illusion to the hanging of the swagman, is actually a phrase used to capture the roving, independent life. To go "Waltzing Matilda" was to sling your few possessions on your back and head for the open road. The song is, therefore, a plea for us to live the unincumbered life.

As a myth, it sounds innocent enough, but it represents a primal human struggle between the landed, tight-fisted elite and the wandering, homeless poor. And it poses the question: "Who really owns the earth, and what purpose does it serve to be the proprietor of anything?" Surely ownership not does confer absolute authority! As one critic of the song wrote in the Yale Review: "Society may require that the squatter shall prevail over the swagman, but the rights of the swagman as a human being must never be forgotten."

While this is a quaint tale for the Aussies, it might just as easily be applied to our own society. Our worth as creatures of God is not measured by the size of our bank accounts. Therefore, those who have nothing are as worthy to receive the fruits of creation as those who have much. Indeed, many religious traditions would suggest that it is only through the recognition of our interdependence which arises out of destitution that we can find eternal blessings.

In this country of balanced budgets and fiscal restraint, we have not solved our problems by reconciling the bottom line. On the contrary, by dismantling the social safety nets as a means to save money, the distinctions between the haves and have-nots are accentuated, and we have simply perpetuated an age-old injustice—pushing the swagman to suicidal acts, so to speak. Shame on us!

SPIRITUALITY: TRUE OR FALSE

It was an innocent examination: grade four, true or false, social studies. Only some of the questions were difficult for my nine-year-old friend Janelle since she is a bright student, alive to the delightful twists and turns of learning. In fact, she would have received a high mark if it weren't for the troubling section on aboriginal peoples.

Among questions of prairie wheat production, the westward spread of white "settlers" across Canada's great plains, there was a simple query. "Natives are superstitious. True or False?" Janelle, apart from resenting the latent racism of the person who would frame such a question, knew quite well that all peoples have indigenous religious beliefs. So she answered "false." Aboriginal peoples are not particularly susceptible to hocus-pocus—no more than any other human community.

The teacher had marked her answer on this question as incorrect. According to this instructor, natives were "superstitious" because they worshipped water and fire, prayed to animals and venerated the moon. There was no question. Even when challenged by Janelle's father, the mark did not change.

I find this piece of class room lore to be frightening for two reasons.

First, the spirituality of the first nations of this continent is no less or more inclined to a magical or fictitious interpretation of the cosmos than any other. A sober look at Christianity reveals that the disciples of Christ hold a number of "superstitious" beliefs: a woman can become pregnant without intercourse, dead people can rise from their tombs, bread and wine can become a divine substance, special sprinklings of water have protective and curative powers. To hold a belief in matters that lack or confound empirical data is not the exclusive territory of one race and to make such a suggestion is biased and unjust. It is from the potent mixture of these false assumptions that ethnic hatred and genocidal war are based.

Second, when one employs the notion of superstition to describe religious propositions, we are ignoring the very real fact that most human beings rely much more heavily on myth than fact when it comes to making the significant decisions over questions of living. Belief does not run contrary to the human quest for fullness, it is essential to it.

All right, what do I mean? Since when did the sober scientific mind of white North American culture give way to "superstition"?

It's easy. We of all peoples are the true believers. For instance, who among us doesn't believe in democracy—the rule of the people with one vote for each individual. And yet even the most optimistic among us would agree that there is little sign that the common will of the people directs public policy. Quite clearly the interests of some segments of society carry more freight, their votes weigh more heavily in the political balance. Alas, democracy is a myth, not a fact. Nevertheless, we live by it faithfully. And can we be faulted for such dedication? Democracy is an inspiring dream.

Similarly, we all have been infected by the romance

virus. As we grow through our adolescence, we live in unswerving expectation that a "true love" is waiting around the corner for each of us. Moreover, once encountered, this once-in-a-lifetime attachment will usher in a relationship marked by days punctuated with enlivening debates and nights filled with sensual backrubs. Oh, we do believe in that true companion! It seems silly when brought into the light of day, but this "superstition" is driving a multi-million-dollar cosmetics industry, the production and distribution of thousands of romance novels, and countless services for single people. And who would want to burst that bubble, if indeed it is that fragile? Even if true and lasting love doesn't actually makes the world go round, its pursuit certainly does.

Myth can't be proven true. Nor is it false. Perhaps we should educate our children to embrace it for what it is— the heart beat of the human soul and the source of our enlightenment.

christopher levan

sin boldly